Reverdy Johnson

The United States, vs. Andrés Castillero on Cross Appeal

Claim for the Mine and Lands of New Almaden

Reverdy Johnson

The United States, vs. Andrés Castillero on Cross Appeal
Claim for the Mine and Lands of New Almaden

ISBN/EAN: 9783337255138

Printed in Europe, USA, Canada, Australia, Japan

Cover: Foto ©Suzi / pixelio.de

More available books at **www.hansebooks.com**

In the United States District Court,

NORTHERN DISTRICT OF CALIFORNIA.

THE UNITED STATES, ⎫
       vs.   ⎬ ON CROSS APPEAL.
ANDRES CASTILLERO. ⎭

Claim for the Mine and Lands of New Almaden

ARGUMENT

OF

Hon. REVERDY JOHNSON,

DELIVERED ON THE

Second and Third Days of November, 1860.

IN REPLY TO THE GOVERNMENT'S SPECIAL COUNSEL.

SAN FRANCISCO:

COMMERCIAL STEAM BOOK AND JOB PRINTING ESTABLISHMENT.

1860.

ARGUMENT.

MR. JOHNSON said:—

May it please your Honors: The magnitude of the interest which the case involves; the many and peculiar questions of law which it presents; the facts on which the claims of our clients rest; their denial; the grounds of that denial; the manner in which these have been maintained; the official character of the personage who has so figured in the contest; its entire history from its origin to the present hour—cause me to feel more than ordinary embarrassment in rising to address your Honors.

That embarrassment is greatly increased by the manner in which my friends and colleagues have discharged their part of the duty imposed upon us all. Presenting to the Court all the learning appropriate to the case, and explaining it with felicitous perspicuity, they have developed the facts and applied the evidence with an acuteness and power which makes me despair of being able to suggest anything having even the *air* of novelty. All that I dare hope is, that I may submit some views which will further assist the deliberations of the Bench.

A professional career, now of nearly half a century, bringing me into immediate connection with almost every variety of official controversy, and an acquaintance from reading, yet more extensive, of such controversies in every civilized land, has never brought to my knowledge a case so conducted as this has been on the part of the Government. So extraordinary has it been, that at times I almost doubted whether I was living under a Government of laws, and breathing the air of Justice and Freedom. The plainest principles of both have been so grossly violated; the claims of suitors so wholly disregarded; the feelings of gentlemen so ruthlessly insulted; the courtesies of life so absolutely forgotten; the comity due to a feeble foreign nation—and because feeble, so shamelessly trampled upon,—that I could hardly credit that it was all done under the sanction of a Government, whose highest duty and special pride it should be to establish an elevated standard of public morality, and to throw wide open all the avenues which might be necessary to the vindication and establishment of truth and justice.

That the agents of a free and enlightened people should use their short-lived power—short-lived as, I thank God, it is—to keep from the Court the truth and the evidence of the truth upon which this case should rest; should entrench themselves behind the laws, real or supposed, of the defense, for the purpose of presenting its discovery to them; and apparently hope, that by such means they might confiscate private property, not to be accomplished if the truth *was* discovered,—would in any Government under the sun be hardly thought credible.

And yet, before I have done, may it please your Honors, I am sorry to say that I hope to show that that has been precisely the conduct of those who have managed this case on the part of the Government.

I rise, may it please your Honors, to aid you in the duty of thwarting such efforts; to assist you in what I am sure is your desire—to do all that in you lies to vindicate the cause of truth and justice, to preserve the good name of our country, to redeem its pledged honor, and to rescue these suitors from the load of scurrilous abuse which the Government has thought proper to heap upon their heads.

My colleagues have anticipated me in the duty; and for the manner of doing it, one of them has received the rebuke of the learned counsel of the Government. His (Mr. Benjamin's) argument was derided, his rhetoric unkindly criticised; throwing aside its alleged insulting reproaches upon the Attorney-General and its alleged appeals to the public, your Honors have been told it was but a repetition of what had long since been *better* said in behalf of his clients by another.

On the special attorney's stricture upon the argument, I have nothing to say. I leave it to the judgment of your Honors. Its power is too fresh in my own recollection to need a word in its support. I leave that part of the reproof without remark.

But, upon the other topic, I cannot refrain from saying that however high my brother's estimate may be of his own professional sense of duty, he sins against all the laws of good taste when he indulges in harsh animadversions upon the conduct of J. P. Benjamin. That gentleman is in my presence. I forbear, therefore, to say of him all that I think and feel. Rich in all the learning that becomes the accomplished lawyer, with a power of argument rarely, if ever, surpassed; his eloquence, yet apparently thrilling through this chamber, delighting, as it did, the ear of the Bench and all who had the happiness to hear it; his uniform courtesy to the Bench and the Bar; his marked regard for the feelings of his adversary; his social qualities and intellectual endowments, that make him the delight of every refined and cultivated circle—will retain for him undiminished the esteem and admiration of all who have the good fortune to know him, although he may not have been able in this instance to have reached that high degree of professional courtesy so strongly recommended and attractively illustrated by the special counsel of the Government! He will continue to be, in despite of that omission which, perhaps, he will never be able to supply in the future, the ornament of the Senate of his country, and the pride and boast of its National Bar.

I have done with this topic, may it please your Honors. I regret, greatly regret, the necessity, which, as I supposed, rendered it necessary to indulge in such reflections.

I proceed to the argument, and I shall endeavor to conduct it with all the mildness that the circumstances will permit.

The propositions which I shall seek to maintain are these:

First. That the claim for the mine is before the Court.

Second. That it is one which your Honors, if you believe the facts on which the claim rests, are bound to confirm under the act by whose authority you are now here, as far as this case is concerned.

And, before stating the other propositions I proceed to argue the preliminary objection involved in these which I have stated.

It is objected by my brother upon the other side, that whatever may have been the purpose of the pleader, he has so inartificially performed his work that he has failed to bring before you for confirmation the mining title of his clients.

This upon the part of my brother, is a modern discovery. It was not made before. The decision of the majority of the Board who confirmed the title, as well as the decision of the third Commissioner who rejected the title, assumed that the claim to the mine was presented for rejection or confirmation. I have stated that it is a modern discovery of the counsel upon the other side; for otherwise I am unable to account for the mass of evidence which, without objection, he has suffered to be taken—and has taken himself—in relation to this very claim, which swells the record up to the size in which your Honors behold it.

And now, at the last moment, when all other efforts have failed, the counsel for the Government, in behalf of the Government, in order to preserve to the Government this property, according to their estimate of incalculable value, rely upon this—I was about to say, *miserable*—technical objection!

Now, the objection, may it please your Honors, involves the mining petition. Was it the purpose of the petition to present the claim? The whole title to the mine is set out with all the particularity necessary to present the claim for adjudication to the tribunal to whom the petition was presented; the very papers that my brother upon the other side alleges are fraudulent, are all there specially referred to and relied upon as the muniments of the title; the continual possession, and the expenditure consequent upon a belief of the title swelling up in amount to $930,000, are alleged; and the petition concludes: (Transcript, page 8)—"And the petitioner relies for confirmation of title upon the original documents, copies of which are transmitted herewith; and upon such other and further proofs as they may be advised are necessary." What title did they expect to be confirmed? The title to the two leagues? Why, that in comparison with the value of the whole matter in dispute was as nothing. The title to the *mine* also, as evidenced by the introduction of all the papers relied upon by the petitioner ; the saving to themselves the expenditure of nearly one million of dollars—"as well as by all other proofs applicable to their title, that they might at any time during the controversy be able to produce."

The Board, all of them first holding that this title was before them, as well as the title to the two leagues, affirmed this title and rejected the title to the two leagues. What was then done by the parties upon the other side ?

From the decision of the Board affirming the title to the mine, the United States took an appeal ; and here is their petition, upon page 132 of the Transcript :

The United States, by their attorney, represent that this cause is for a review of the decision of the U. S. Land Commission, whereby the claim of the Appellee was confirmed in part, as will appear by reference to the record in the case; that a transcript of said record was filed in this Court, Feb. 26, 1856; that a notice of appeal was filed on the part of the United States, April 15, 1856; that the land claimed lies in this District, and that said claim is invalid.

Wherefore appellants pray that this Court reverse the decision of the said Commission, and decree the said claim invalid.

The answer to that petition, intended to take issue upon the facts presented in that petition of appeal, is found on page 142 of the Transcript; and it reads thus :

That his titles to the mine and lands of New Almaden, as set forth and described in his petition to the Board of Commissioners, and in the documentary and other evidence filed in this case, are good and valid titles; that the land, property and interest so claimed by him are situate in the Northern District of California, and within the jurisdiction of this Court.

And he prays this honorable Court to affirm so much of the decision of the Commissioners as confirms his said claim.

This is immediately followed by a notice on the part of the

United States, signed by the then District Attorney of the United States, to the appellee, to produce certain papers, with which it is unnecessary to trouble the Court by reading; all of which papers relate to the title to the mine.

And that is followed by a further notice, upon page 198 of the Transcript, for an additional production of papers, some ten or fifteen in number ; all of which relate to the mine.

The papers are produced for the second time as evidence; so offered, so given. The case is now for hearing. Not a whisper of objection fell from the lips of the counsel for the United States, that the whole of this evidence had nothing to do with the case before the Court. If they had thought so, may it please your Honors, they ought to have demurred to the petition.

But where does my brother find that any petition is necessary ? The language of the Act of 1851 requires no petition. The 8th section says that " Each and every person claiming, etc., shall present the same to the said Commissioners." Whether it is to be done in the form of a petition, or by the presentation of the title papers upon which the claim rests, the statute says nothing. It could not be tolerated in a Court of last resort, upon an appeal from a judgment pronounced upon an issue admitted on all sides to have been before the Court, to adjudicate on each of every supposed or real defect, if the objection had not been made at the time. It is a rule of universal practice necessary to the performance of justice, that an appellate tribunal will not permit an objection to be taken before itself for the first time, which, if taken in the Court below, might be corrected. I cite no authorities for such a principle of elementary law.

But, may it please your Honors, have you no power to authorize an amendment ? You are an appellate Court; an appeal from the decision of the Commissioners is given to you as a Court. You look to the constitution of this tribunal— to what made your powers here as a Court—in acting; and in the absence of an express or implied restriction upon your authority to amend, that authority exists in every case, and of course in this. And the result is, that if there was any foundation at all for the objection that occurred to the special attorney, the Court would direct the prayer of the petition, in that respect, to be amended. Would it not be amended, may it please the Court, if it was an ordinary case of equity pleading ?

The case of the petitioner is made out in his petition. The supposed defect is not making the prayer for relief coextensive with the necessities of his case, as the case is presented ; he makes one prayer, which does not cover his entire claim. Your Honors will not permit the mistake of counsel, not called to the attention of the Court below, when they could, and would have been corrected, if called to the Court's attention below, to injure the client in the appellate tribunal, but direct at once the amendment to be made. My brother upon the other side would have saved himself an immense deal of labor ; saved his intellect an immense deal of wear and tear ; he need not have subjected himself to the intellectual trial between himself and the Mexican witnesses, nor have pursued the game he attempted to play with my colleague, as a witness, if the case was not before the Court—unless he is much more fond of labor than lawyers generally are.

Well, now, may it please your Honors, if the claim is before you, the next question under this head is : Is it a claim that can be legitimately before you under the provisions of the Act of 1851 ?

How is that Act to be construed, if there is any doubt upon its face in this or any other particular ? To solve the doubt, where the objection in the particular case is, that it does not cover a case intended to be provided for by the treaty, you go to the treaty. And, if going to the treaty, you discover that the case before the Court was intended to be embraced by the treaty, then, although the words of the act passed for the purpose of carrying the treaty into execution may be doubtful, you give them a construction to cover everything that the treaty was intended to protect.

What was the treaty intended to protect? Private property of *every description* belonging to Mexicans, or to anybody else, derived from the Mexican Government, having its origin in Mexican law, depending for its validity upon Mexican jurisprudence and common law statute. And why? Because, in this enlightened age of the world, nobody has ever supposed that there was any foundation for the principle which the coarse intellect of Bynkershoek thought proper to announce—that private property could be destroyed, either by conquest or by cession.

It is not necessary to inquire into the effect of conquest, because, in this particular, there is no conquest. It is only necessary to see what the Government of the United States have undertaken to do. Have they by their treaty intended to protect every species of property known to the laws of Mexico, and valuable in point of fact?

ARTICLE 8.—Mexicans now established in territories previously belonging to Mexico, and which remain for the future within the limits of the United States, as defined by the present treaty, shall be free to continue where they now reside, or to remove at any time to the Mexican Republic, retaining the property which they possess in the said territories, or disposing thereof, and removing the proceeds wherever they please, without their being subjected, on this account, to any contribution, tax, or charge whatever.

Those who shall prefer to remain in the said territories, may either retain the title and rights of Mexican citizens, or acquire those of citizens of the United States. But they shall be under the obligation to make their election within one year from the date of the exchange of ratifications of this treaty; and those who shall remain in the said territories after the expiration of that year, without having declared their intention to retain the character of Mexicans, shall be considered to have elected to become citizens of the United States.

In the said territories, property of every kind, now belonging to Mexicans not established there, shall be inviolably respected.—The present owners, the heirs of these, and all Mexicans who may hereafter acquire said property by contract, shall enjoy with respect to it guaranties equally ample as if the same belonged to citizens of the United States.

We present the claim to a mine. We say the title was derived from Mexico. We produce the title papers, and establish by proof—as far as this part of the argument is concerned—to be assumed as true, and as evidence of such title. My learned brother upon the other side, and the dissenting

Commissioner before the Board, maintained that it is a case not covered by the Act of 1851. That it was embraced by the treaty, if there could be any doubt from the language and words of the treaty, is admitted by Mr. Commissioner Thompson. That part of his opinion is at page 127 of the Transcript. He tells us, "That a compliance with the terms of the ordinance would give *a right of property in the mine*, which the treaty of Guadalupe Hidalgo *would protect*, if the law in which that right is founded is not abrogated by the act of cession, does not admit of controversy."

I have a right, therefore, to assume it as true, that if this is *property*, it is protected by the treaty; and the only question for your Honors to decide is: Is it covered by the act of 1851 —under whose authority you are acting?

That act was passed to carry into effect the provisions of that treaty; and so far as relates to real property, is undisputed. With personal property it did not interfere. It left the title to personal property to be decided by the local Courts, under the authority of the general jurisprudence of the State, or of the United States. But the United States, with reference to real property, or interest in real property, had a policy of its own. That policy in relation to similar treaties was carried out by the act of 1824, and the antecedent acts passed under provisions to carry into effect the treaties with Spain and with France. All that time Congress thought that it was not necessary to provide any particular mode of passing upon titles derived from Spain or from France during the period that the territories ceded were the property either of Spain or of France, where those titles were consummated so as to vest in their owners an estate in fee which could be maintained in Courts of Justice by ordinary proceedings; but that it *was* necessary to provide for all cases of inchoate titles which, at the date of the several treaties that those acts were passed in relation to, had gone to such an extent as to bind, at the moment of the cession, the conscience of the former Government.

California, it was imagined, with reference to these titles, was in a different condition. It was a distinct province of Mexico; sparsely populated. The United States did not know the possible extent of the titles—the real and consummated titles—and of course did not know to what extent the domain ceded by Mexico had been converted before the cession into private estate. They made, therefore, the Act of 1851 more extensive than the provisions of the antecedent legislation in relation to other treaties; and the policy of that course upon the part of the Government, is stated by the Chief Justice—Taney—in the case of Fremont vs. The United States, to be found at page 542, 17 Howard's Reports. I read from page 553. After speaking of the acts passed in relation to the cessions of Louisiana and Florida, the Chief Justice says:

The laws of Congress giving the jurisdiction, were different in one respect, and the condition of the countries, as well as the *laws and usages* of the nation making the grants, were also different. It will be seen from the quotation we have made, that the 8th section embraces not only inchoate or equitable titles, but legal titles also; and requires them all to undergo examination, and to be passed upon by the Court. The object of this provision appears to be to place the *titles* to land in California upon a stable foundation, and to give to the parties who *possess* them an opportunity of placing them on the records of the country, in a manner and form that will prevent future controversy.

Now what have they done? The 8th section of the Act of 1851 provides that "Each and every person claiming lands in California by virtue of any right or title derived from the Spanish or Mexican Government, shall present the same to the said Commissioners when sitting as a board, together with such documentary evidence and testimony of witnesses as the said claimant relies upon in support of such claims; and it shall be the duty of the Commissioners, when the case is ready for hearing, to proceed promptly to examine the same upon such evidence, and upon the evidence produced in behalf of the United States, and to decide upon the validity of the said claim, and, within thirty days after such decision is rendered, to certify the same, with the reasons on which it is founded, to the District Attorney of the United States in and for the district in which such decision shall be rendered."

The 11th section provides "That the Commissioners herein

provided for, and the District and Supreme Courts, in deciding on the validity of any claim brought before them under the provisions of this act, shall be governed by the treaty of Guadalupe Hidalgo, the law of nations, the laws, usages and customs of the government from which the claim is derived, the principles of equity, and the decisions of the Supreme Court of the United States, so far as they are applicable."

Well, all that it is necessary to do, may it please your Honors, is to show that the particular claim is derived from Mexico; that the title set up and asked to be confirmed is a title, in the language of the act, "derived from the Spanish or Mexican Government."

Now, it is said that it was not the purpose of the act to cover a mining title. It is admitted to have been the object of the *treaty*, but it is not the design of that *act*, because it is not a claim to *lands !* And we have had a brilliant metaphysical discussion on the part of my brother on the other side, to tell us what lands *are*, and what lands are *not ;* and he arrived at the very satisfactory conclusion that a quarter-dollar thrown on the surface of the land, was not land. Well, *that* I can see.

He said, in the opening of the case upon the part of the Government, that the act covered only an *absolute interest* in land; the *fee simple*, as contradistinguished from any lesser title. He must go to that extent, or the whole argument fails. Then, if by the laws of Mexico there could be in the real estate of Mexico estates for life, estates for years, estates in *fee tail*, estates in *fee simple conditional*, as these several estates are known to the Common Law of England and the United States, the moment the country was ceded to the United States they all became vested *in* the United States. Property in Mexico—an interest in lands in Mexico—to be recovered by the ordinary proceedings provided by the laws of Mexico for the recovery of interest in real estate—liable to sale in Mexico—liable to be forfeited as real estate in Mexico, was not within the treaty, or, if within the treaty, not within this statute!

I have shown you that it was the object of the treaty to protect every kind of interest in real estate. Now, suppose this Act of 1851 is doubtful in any particular instance. There

is one consideration which would force your Honors to come
to the conclusion to which we invite you, and that is this : that
all claims to land not confirmed by this act, under the provisions of this law, by the Board of Land Commissioners, if not
appealed from—by the decision of the District Court, if that
be not appealed from—by the final decision of the Supreme
Court of the United States, where there is an appeal—shall become a part of the public domain of the United States. Then
my brother would have you to believe that the Congress of the
United States, with the faith of the nation pledged to protect
every claim derived by any kind of title from Mexico, intended so cunningly to devise their statute as to confiscate—
for aught that your Honors can know—to the United States,
more than one-half of the claims to land in California derived
from titles given by Mexico.

But to apply it to the particular case. The mine, says Mr.
Attorney General and his representative here, is of inestimable
value; it has yielded already eight millions of dollars to its
possessors, with which they ought to be satisfied—according to
him—if they are permitted to go free, instead of having the
money taken from them, and spending the rest of their lives in
the penitentiary ! Beautiful language *that* for an officer of the
Government! Some of them would not look well in that place !
The Attorney General tells us that arithmetic can hardly cal-
culate the value—of what? Of this *estate*. *He* does not pretend to say it is not an estate in land. Of this *mine*. *He* does
not pretend to say that, if the title is in us, it is not protected
by the treaty. *He* does not set up the objection that the Act of
1851 does not embrace it. I will do *him* the justice to say
that. But his representative here tells your Honors, that although it be of such value, and although our alleged right to
hold it, is a right derived from the laws of Mexico, under a title
justified by the laws of Mexico, it is one that we cannot get
confirmed under the provisions of this Act of 1851 ; because
the Act of 1851 has left out so much of the property intended
to be secured by the treaty of 1848 !

Could you give it that interpretation, may it please your
Honors, even if you supposed it to be doubtful ? No ; cer-

tainly not. I am addressing myself to just men, anxious, determined to preserve the good faith of our common nation; and I have no doubt, therefore—not the slightest—that your Honors will hold with the majority of the Board by whom the title to this mine was confirmed, that it *is* within the provisions of the Act of 1851.

But the Supreme Court have told you, in a decision pronounced the term before the last in Fossatt's case (which was supposed to involve the claim to this mine), what was the object of the treaty, and the object of the act of 1851. I read from page 448, 21st Howard's Reports:

These acts of Congress do not create a voluntary jurisdiction that the claimant may seek or decline. * * * * This jurisdiction comprehends *every species of title or right, whether inchoate or complete;* whether resting in contract or evinced by authentic act and judicial possession. The object of this inquiry was *not to discover forfeitures or to enforce rigorous conditions.* The declared purpose was to authenticate *titles,* and to afford the solid guarantee to *rights* which ensues from their full acknowledgment by the supreme authority.

So at pages 450 and 451:

The United States did not appear in the Courts as a *contentious litigant.*

They are reproving in advance those who have managed this case. They (the United States) did not appear in the Courts as a contentious litigant. But how did they appear?

As a great nation, acknowledging their obligation to recognize as valid *every authentic title.*

And what else? By closing up the doors by which evidence was to be obtained for and against the title? By denouncing the whole Mexican Nation, and asking your Honors to presume, as a presumption of law—taught to you as a jury,—that they are all false swearers—equal in that respect to all the swearers of Catholic Christendom? No, may it please your Honors; but "ACKNOWLEDGING THEIR OBLIGATION TO RECOGNIZE AS VALID EVERY AUTHENTIC TITLE, AND SOLICITING EXACT INFORMATION

TO DIRECT THEIR EXECUTIVE GOVERNMENT TO COMPLY WITH THAT OBLIGATION."

Mr. Attorney General, when he wrote the letter to which I will call your Honors' attention by and by, and when he wrote his opinion in relation to California titles in general, and the New Almaden title in particular, had not read that lesson upon national morality taught us by the Supreme Court of the United States.

Now, may it please your Honors, the title being before you for judgment, the next question, and the only question which can excite any interest, or could excite any interest—in the public mind at least, and in that of the Court,—is: Whether that title was fairly acquired or not?

We have in these pleadings, repeated over and over again in the argument, the charge of FALSE; FRAUDULENT; FORGED; FABRICATED. Not satisfied with applying all these epithets to it, it was also "antedated!" And then, as a legal conclusion—for the pleader seemed to think the Court would not see that that was the result of the charge, if made good,—it was, because it was "false, forged, fraudulent and fabricated," null and of no effect.

Now, I propose, may it please the Court, very briefly—for the whole ground has been so well covered by my colleagues, that I am satisfied it is quite unnecessary—to examine into the truth of these charges.

There are some things about which the counsel on the other side and ourselves do not differ. We start from them, therefore, as common ground.

There was a man—I believe my friend on the other side admits there was such a man in existence once as Andres Castillero. There was such a man as this petitioner—and probably is now; he is not "forged;" and he is not "fabricated" for these purposes. That same man was here in 1845. He was a Mexican; conversant with the science of mining (if it be a science); anxious to show his skill; glad in that way, not only to promote his own interest, but to promote the interest of his country; and, in the latter part of 1845, he had discovered this mine. That is admitted.

Mr. Randolph—Discovered the quicksilver in it.

Mr. Johnson—Well, that is the same thing. "Mine" and "quicksilver" are synonymous terms. What is his belief, may it please your Honors? That he thought it exceedingly valuable. How valuable? More valuable than the Almaden mine of Spain—and *its* value could hardly be counted at that time in dollars. What did he think when he discovered it? That it would be a very good thing to make it his own private property, if it could be accomplished. But he had no means of his own; and the very first step that he took, evidenced by any authentic written act, was executing a contract of partnership (which bears date November 2, 1845), by which he takes with him as partners General José Castro, Secundino and Teodoro Robles, and Padre Real.

This contract of partnership, my brother on the other side admits, was made on or about the 2d of November, 1845. It is therefore an authentic paper. What did it look to? The working of this mine. The first article says:

"Don Andres Castillero, conforming in all respects to the Ordinance of Mining, forms a regular perpetual partnership with the said persons in this form;" and then goes on to state the terms of the partnership.

Now, he has discovered the mine; he values it highly; he enters in good faith, on the 2d of November, 1845, into a contract of partnership to work it. What else did he do, about which there can be no dispute?

He knew that there were mining laws in Mexico, in force here, under which the individual discoverer could secure to himself the mine discovered. What would he be likely to do? To proceed according to such laws. What do we say he did? Denounced and registered the mine; wrote to Mexico, where at last his title was to be confirmed; sent specimens of the ore there. What for? To prepare the authorities in whom was vested the power to confer upon him the title, for the application which he contemplated making, to get the title. He goes to Mexico; and being in Mexico, the discoverer of the mine or denouncer of the mine, what would he have done in all probability? Taken the steps in Mexico necessary to secure the title.

Where would these carry him? To the very Department of the Government of Mexico, in which we say he appeared. What would he do when he got there? Precisely what we say he did.

Well, then, it is clear, may it please your Honors; no man can doubt, because every man, placed in his condition, feels that he would have done the same thing; that the very acts, which we maintain as established upon evidence upon which the mind cannot doubt, were done by the discoverer of this mine, were the very acts that any man in his senses, situated as he was, would have done.

Now, what did he do—as we say, before he went to Mexico? An official communication, dated the 21st of April, 1846, was made by the Junta de Fomento to General Tornel, Director of the National College of Mining, sending specimens for assay with copies of Castillero's letters to Herrera and Moral. That is, before he arrived. How these are proved, I will tell the Court by-and-by. The minutes of the proceedings of the *Junta Facultativa* of the College, of the 24th of April, 1846, (dated in point of fact, the 24th of *March*, but evidently should be dated the 24th of *April*), prove what I have stated.

An official communication, dated 29th of April, from Tornel, Director of the College, to Moral, President of the Junta Facultativa, acknowledges the receipt of a letter from Moral of the 24th of April, 1846, communicating the result of the assay.

In an official communication, dated the 29th of April, 1846, from Tornel, the Director of the College, to the Junta de Fomento, was communicated the result of the assay.

In an official communication, dated the 5th of May, 1846, from the Junta de Fomento to the Minister of Justice, the discovery of Castillero was made known to the President.

On the 12th of May, 1846, Castillero proposed to the Junta to contract for the working of the mine.

On the 14th of May, 1846, there was an official communication from the Junta to the Minister of Justice, announcing the original foregoing contract, and urgently recommending the President of the Republic to agree to it.

On the 20th of May, 1846, an official communication from

the Minister of Justice to the Junta de Fomento ratifies and approves said contract in all its parts.

An official communication of the 20th of May, 1846, from the Minister of Justice to the Minister of Relations, communicating the President's approval of Castillero's contract with the Junta de Fomento, and grant of two square leagues on the land of his mining possession, directs the Minister of Relations to issue the proper orders.

On the 23d of May, 1846, the orders referred to in that communication, are stated to have been issued.

On the 23d of May, 1846, in an official communication addressed by the Minister of Relations to the Governor of the Department of California, setting forth the President's approval of Castillero's contract, and grant of two square leagues on his mining possession, the Governor is ordered to put him in possession of said land ?

That is the two league grant.

So your Honors see, if these things actually occurred, they are precisely what Castillero would have endeavored to obtain after making the discovery of this mine and going to Mexico —where the title, through this instrumentality, could be consummated.

Now, my brother says that these papers—and several others to which I shall have occasion to advert by-and-by—were all forged, fabricated, false, fraudulent, antedated. He says so still.

> " A man convinced against his will,
> Is of the same opinion still."

Now, may it please your Honors, how are you to approach the consideration of this question of fraud and falsehood upon the part of a claimant who produces evidence of the official act of a foreign Government ?

In the case of Arredondo, Mr. Justice Baldwin, speaking for the Supreme Court, laid down two rules which he said were incontrovertible. The first was : That actual fraud is not to be presumed; but is to be *proved*. By whom? By the party who alleges it. Second : That, if the motive and design of an act may be traced to an honest, legitimate source, equally as to a corrupt one, the former should be preferred.

The United States now are for reversing these two rules. They ask us to prove in advance of other proof in relation to the production of the documents of title derived from the admitted authorities of Mexico, that they are *not* false, and fraudulent, and forged, and fabricated! There is no such rule known to justice or to morals. The burthen of proving the fraud is, in this case, on the Government, who asserts it. The obligation on the claimant is complied with when he produces his *prima facie* evidence of his title; consisting in the archives in which, he says, the title is to be found recorded; authenticated by the acts of the public officers of the Government from whom the title was derived. In this case he has gone infinitely further. He has produced here the very officers themselves, to prove that all these titles were fairly and honestly obtained. When was that done? About eighteen months ago. Before then, may it please your Honors, we had, as I think, evidence enough to have put the United States upon the inquiry as to the authenticity of our documentary title. Our Minister in Mexico, Mr. Forsyth, a man whose integrity nobody will question, had stated that he had examined into all those archives; that the copies we produce he knew to have been fairly copied from the originals on file; and that he saw—to use his own language—" no reason whatever to doubt the integrity of the entire transaction."

But the property is a large one. The title so authenticated is alleged to be defectively proved! The taint of fraud is still upon it, in the estimation of the counsel for the Government, here and in Washington. The character of these gentlemen (the claimants) is still unrelieved. Fortunately for them they had the means of producing additional evidence, calculated, as they supposed, as their counsel supposed, as everybody else supposed—except the counsel for the United States—to place the charge entirely beyond the scope of belief. They g) to Mexico; they examine for themselves into the archives; they succeed, at a great expense, in inducing some of the officials who were engaged in these several offices at the time the transactions took place, to come to San Francisco with the means of identifying the truth of these documents beyond all possible

doubt—provided they told the truth; provided they were entitled to be credited. Here, they come. What it cost to bring
them, your Honors have already heard. Here, they are examined. Here, my brother meets them. Here, he propounds
his four thousand or five thousand questions, more or less.
Here, days and weeks and months are exhausted in trying to
establish the fact—which he suspected to be true—that the
whole story which they were here to defend is a false and
fraudulent story.

We have been represented in Mexico since, if not by a Minister Plenipotentiary, by a Consul in the City of Mexico, disposed to obey the orders of his Government, because disobey-
ing a clear official duty under the Act of Congress—when
called upon to take testimony—in consequence of an order of
his Government; and no evidence has been produced during
the year that has elapsed since these witnesses were examined,
to satisfy your Honors that any single word of their testimony
is false, according to the story told by the archives as they
exist in the City of Mexico. Have these been examined, may
it please your Honors? My brother upon the other side writes
—as he told you yesterday or the day before—letter after
letter to the Attorney General and to the assistant counsel in
Washington, begging them to send to Mexico for the purpose
of discovering there the fraud. Did not he (the Attorney General) suppose that THERE the evidence of the fraud could be
obtained?

MR. RANDOLPH—I desired to send to Mexico for the purpose of getting proof of the fraud in a convenient shape to be
used in a criminal case.

MR. JOHNSON—I understand that; but still it is a proof of
the fraud.

Has it been done? My brother says—nobody has a right to
doubt him; certainly I do not—that, as far as he knows, it has
not been done. One of two things is true: it has been, or it
has not; about that we cannot differ.

If it has not, are we not entitled to the whole benefit of the inference to be drawn from the fact that the United States have not ventured to make the inquiry ?

If it has been done, and the inquiry has resulted in establishing the truth of these archives, the non-production to your Honors of the result of that inquiry tells, as against the United States, a story that I should be very unwilling to believe.

There is in this record, may it please your Honors, a correspondence between some of the counsel for these claimants and Mr. Attorney General. I am sure the Court will read the whole of it, before they proceed to dispose of this case. We knew what the charge was here. We had absolute conviction that there was not the slightest foundation for it. We had the assurance which the high character of these gentlemen of itself gave, strengthened, as it was with reference to ourselves individually, from the intimate personal relations of friendship which subsisted between some of them and ourselves; and we invoked, in their behalf, the Government to take such steps as would satisfy them, so that these gentlemen might be freed from the influence in public opinion that charges coming from the United States could not help more or less to create. " We propose," says Mr. Attorney General, in his reply to our communication on the 8th of March, 1859 (and your Honors will find that letter at page 2939), "a variety of ways in which the Government could convince themselves whether their suspicious were well or ill founded." Mr. Attorney General says, in writing to the President, to whom we were obliged finally to make a direct appeal, that the counsel for the claimants propose one of five things:

First. Direct the counsel of the United States to *consent* that the copies of certain papers in the claimant's possession shall be admitted in evidence.

Second. Order them to adopt some measure which will satisfy themselves that these copies are correctly taken.

Third. Order them to procure other copies of the same papers, in such manner and by such agent as they may select.

Fourth. Solicit of the Mexican Government the original papers relating to Castillero's transactions with it concerning this grant; or,

Fifth. Ask of Mexico a copy of all such papers, authenticated by the great seal of the Republic.

One of the modes that we proposed was—not believing it possible that *that* could be rejected—to select any gentlemen of intelligence and character that they pleased ; let them go as a Commission to Mexico and examine the archives ; and let them come down to San Francisco and testify here before the Court the result of the search. Let the Minister do it, who was then at the City of Mexico, we said. If, from his official station, he was unable to accomplish it, send out the Commission ! Make the selection of Commissioners yourselves ! If attended by an extraordinary expense, which the Executive of the United States would not permit them to incur, our clients will pay the expense!

We offered it with no offensive view. We believed that it was barely possible that Mr. Attorney General, or the President of the United States, might be under the impression that there was no fund in the Treasury to bear the expenditure which would be incurred by such a Commission. We said, therefore, send it out, and our clients will incur the whole expenditure ; substantially, we will treat the Commissioners as we had to treat those Mexican witnesses—we will carry them to Mexico in the best possible way ; we will see them taken care of in Mexico in the best possible mode ; we will bring them to California ; we will pay their expenses in the most liberal manner ; we will pay them for their time. If it costs $200,000, we are willing to give it to American gentlemen, selected by the Government for the purpose of discovering into the truth of this alleged charge of fraud upon the part of the Government.

We said, in the conclusion of one of the letters: " And here we beg to be permitted to say, there is no form in which our Government can request or exact from that of Mexico the assurance of the latter as to the genuineness of these papers, which we will not cheerfully acquiesce in." That is as far back as the 19th of November, 1858. It was received by us in Washington on or about the 17th of December, 1858 ; and it was communicated by us to the authorities at Washington on that day—the letter communicating it being signed by Mr. Benjamin and myself, and by J. J. Crittenden and John A. Rockwell (page 2929). That is to the Secretary of State.

My friend, the Secretary of State, got it, but he did not answer it for a good while. I suppose he put it in the hands of the Attorney General, and *he* could *not* answer it. But he *does* answer that proposition, and the several additional propositions that were made. And how does he answer them, may it please your Honors? Page 2939 :

I. The counsel of the United States cannot possibly consent to the admission of evidence which they believe to be corrupt and false.

That is before it is obtained !

In this case they do believe that the copies of the papers produced by the claimant before the Land Commissioners, and in the Circuit Court, are not satisfactorily authenticated—

So that your Honors could not receive them as testimony at all!

—and they further believe that the originals are themselves fraudulent fabrications. Of course we make it a point of conscience and principle to oppose evidence of that kind.

That is not all.

II. The counsel of the United States (not my brother, because he says *he* has *not* done it; not the former District Attorney, for if he had done it, the testimony would have been here; not the present District Attorney, for he has not had time to do it, and he won't have much time to do it)—the counsel of the United States *have* adopted (what I emphasize, may it please your Honors, is italicized in the letter, and the letter is printed from an official copy of the letter in the Department of State ; so the italics are the italics of the Attorney General, when he handed the letter to the Department of State)—the counsel of the United States *have* adopted very careful measures to *satisfy* themselves concerning these copies, as well as the originals from which they purport to be taken.

What "careful measures" did they take?

MR. RANDOLPH—Inspected the face of the papers, I suppose.

MR. JOHNSON—By the face of the papers you could not well

tell, I suppose. You might suspect, might do as my brother does—indulge in suspicion throughout.

What are we to infer from this, may it please your Honors? What we wanted was to ascertain what the archives in Mexico disclose? The evidence of fraud was *there*, if there *was* fraud. The papers fabricated were *there*, if there *was* fabrication. *There*, we asked them to go. *There*, they virtually say they will *not* go again, for they have been there already. They have examined the archives already. The result of the inquiry was, to satisfy them that the originals, there on file, are fraudulent. Give us—

MR. RANDOLPH—(interrupting). I do not understand that the Attorney General makes any such assertion.

MR. JOHNSON—Of course he does not say it. But he has " *satisfied* " himself and " taken very careful measures " to do it. No man in his senses could say that measures necessary to satisfy the mind on a subject of that sort, are not to be taken in the City of Mexico. He is a high official person—the Attorney General of the United States! Every word that *he* says, then, must be true! He has " taken careful measures "! Why did not he let your Honors see what the measures were? Who is the agent in Mexico that made the search? Was it the Consul? Who is the agent sent there for the purpose of making the search? Was it the former District Attorney, Mr. Inge? Let us know what was done. Your Honors are asked to denounce these papers as fraudulent, and to brand the parties concerned with infamy, on the *ex parte* charge of Mr. Attorney General, and the counsel for the United States; and here we are told by the Attorney General himself, that he has adopted measures which have " *satisfied* " him that the charge is well founded; yet he does not dare to lay before the Court what the measures were!

But that is not all. He goes on further to say:

III. You are requested by those gentlemen (Crittenden, Benjamin, Rockwell, and myself) to get other copies of the same papers. In answer to this, I have nothing to say of the unprecedented and singular attitude which the Government would take in sending its own counsel to hunt up the evidence of a hostile claim in favor of Mexican citizens at the seat of the Mexican Government.

That is to say, may it please your Honors, to make the treaty effectual; to preserve the pledged word of the country; to keep her in the estimation of the nations of the world free from reproach; to guard her against claiming for herself property belonging to citizens deriving title from Mexico, when the question is presented for judicial determination—that the property becomes ours unless the claimant can succeed in establishing that it is his. We will not go to Mexico, or suffer anybody else to go to Mexico, for the purpose of searching where alone a search can be made successfully into the fact—because that would be to aid "a hostile claim," as against the United States! "A hostile claim!"

The Supreme Court thought differently, in the opinion I read you just now—the decision of Mr. Justice Campbell in the Fossatt case. Of the very act which Mr. Attorney General announces is "unprecedented," Mr. Justice Campbell, speaking for the Supreme Court of the United States, says: "It is their duty to solicit exact information to direct our Executive Government to comply with the obligation imposed upon them as a great nation by which they have acknowledged their obligation to recognize as valid *every* authentic title." (Page 451, 21st vol. Howard.)

Well, that is not all, may it please your Honors. Mr. Attorney General continues:

But there is another reason which cannot be got over. We want to save the property for ourselves; and that is reason enough! But if that is not sufficient, there is another reason which cannot be successfully met. We will therefore let the first reason pass.

In the language of Mr. Attorney General, "Let that pass!"

But there is another reason which cannot be got over. It is not of the copies alone that we complain. The originals, or some of them at least, may be among the Mexican archives;

and what we assert is, that they were not honestly placed there by the Mexican officers.

All of them may be, or if not all, some of them may be there; but "they were not placed there honestly by the Mexican officers!" They were placed there by the Mexican officers; but "not honestly!" How does he know they were there? all, or one, or any less than all? Because he has made the inquiry. He has had the search conducted by somebody in whom the Government has confidence! It is not Mr. Frederick Billings; no Mexican lawyer employed by Mr. Billings; no Eustace Barron. "In some way *satisfactory* to ourselves, we have made such a careful search that we are rather inclined to believe that the originals of all the papers presented before the Court establishing the title to be confirmed, are in the Mexican archives; but we won't let them be produced. They shall not be authenticated; they shall not be used as evidence if they are not authenticated, so as to make them legal evidence by force of the authentication—because I, Mr. Attorney General, say, in the face of the world, that they were placed there by the Mexican officials dishonestly."

And he gives another reason. His sense of morality is not as yet exhausted.

IV. The next proposition is, that you *solicit* the Mexican Government to furnish *original* papers relating to the claim of Castillero. I concede it to be true, as a rule of public law, that a document which belongs to the Mexican archives, cannot properly reach our judicial tribunals, so as to be noticed by them, except through that Department of our Government which manages its foreign affairs. But this being true, why does not the Republic of Mexico offer the document in question to the Department of State? Why should we take the initiative in reference to the claim of Mexican citizens against ourselves? Or why should we expose the truth,—"(which he says was *falsehood* and *forgery* in the fabrication of the papers)" —to the danger of being perverted by the diplomatic maneuvers which might be resorted to by our opponents?

Is it not evident, may it please your Honors, that the Attorney General thought that the United States, in a case of this description, was to appear in the courts as a "contentious litigant"?

My opinion is, that the Government of the United States should wait until that of Mexico shall make a voluntary tender of the papers which support this title.

What is he going to do with them after he gets them? Why, *that* depends on what they may turn out to be. Is that it? If they will defeat the hostile claim set up by Mexican citizens, as against the United States, we will let them be forthcoming; "if not, we will then decide what we will do with them."

My opinion is, that the Government of the United States should wait until that of Mexico shall make a voluntary tender of the papers which support this title, and then examine into their character with great care, holding Mexico to the full measure of the responsibility she will incur by any aid she may willfully give in the support of a false claim against the United States.

He assumes the fraud and falsehood of the claim, and states here by way of threat: "don't you send us these original papers! It is not *our* duty to ask for them. It is *your* duty, if there is any duty on the subject at all, to send them. But take care how you send them; because, if you do it without being asked, and it establishes the validity of what we say is a false claim, we will hold you to a rigid responsibility, and take another portion of Mexico to make up, by way of indemnity, for this past transaction."

But that is not all. He says he won't ask Mexico to attach the Great Seal, because, if there is any law preventing the use of the Great Seal for any such purpose, it exists by virtue only of a Presidential decree, and that decree may be altered at the will of the Executive. Then he says, after dropping the question of fraud—and I ask your Honor's particular attention to this—(page 2941-'42 of Transcript):

"The Mexican Government, after strict inquiry and examination, having in the most solemn manner, and under the most impressive circumstances, affirmed to the Government of the

United States, that no grant whatever of lands in the territory of California, had been made after the 13th of May, 1846, with what face can that Government now assert the contrary? with what regard to common propriety can the United States ask the Republic of Mexico to do this thing; to violate her own honor, to falsify her own declaration, and to break her solemn pledge after procuring an advantageous treaty of peace upon the faith of it? If it be said that the declaration of the Mexican Commissioners was a mistake, and that a private person should not be compelled to suffer by it, the answer is very plain. He should seek redress from the nation which inflicted the injury. Let him look to his own Government, which pledged its honor that no such grant existed, and not to the United States, who took the pledge as true. Castillero, like every Mexican citizen, was bound by the affirmation which his Government made."

The Supreme Court tells us, that by the law of nations, by the principles now universally admitted as just among the civilized nations of the world, no nation can, in ceding its territory, dispose of the private property acquired by valid title from it before the cession; and your Honor, the District Judge, in an opinion of the ability of which I forbear to speak in the presence in which I stand, has stated that it is not in the power of the Government of Mexico to deprive an individual proprietor, whether a Mexican or somebody else, of land held under Mexico, antecedent to the actual cession, by any declaration which they may have made; and that with reference to the particular declaration relied upon, it is entitled to no consideration whatever, because that article of the treaty—inserted in the original treaty in order to carry out the object of that declaration—was stricken out by the Senate.

Hear how his Honor Judge Hoffman disposes of that objection in this case. I read from the decision of the Court in the United States *vs.* Palmer *et al.*:

On the whole, we are of opinion that the right to grant her public domain in California, continued until the conquest of the country by the United States.

The declaration of war did not take from her the power to grant.

It is further urged, on the part of the United States, that grants made after the 13th of May, are not protected by the treaty of peace, because such was not the intention of the parties. That the Mexican Commissioners who negotiated the peace, and who represented the claimants as well as the Mexican Government, solemnly, and after special inquiry, declared that none such existed.

That the treaty was negotiated on the faith of this declaration.

It is admitted that such a declaration was made and embodied in the *projet* of the treaty submitted to the Senate.

Had this declaration been contained in the treaty, as adopted and ratified, it might very possibly have been regarded as a covenant or stipulation that no such grants should be deemed valid by the United States.

But the clause containing it was struck out by the Senate, not by the general vote which struck out the whole of the 10th article of which this declaration formed a part, but by a distinct vote upon the question whether this particular clause should stand as a part of the treaty. The Court cannot assume, therefore, that the treaty was assented to by the United States on the faith of this declaration by Mexico, else why strike it out?

It may not unreasonably be supposed that the Senate refused to allow the declaration to remain.

Why, your Honor speaks from the inspiration of that Heavenly spirit to which my brother on the other side at the beginning of his argument referred.

It may not unreasonably be supposed that the Senate refused to allow the declaration to remain, because they were willing that grants made *after* the 13th of May, if any such there were, should be submitted to the Courts, and rejected or confirmed, as might be just. But, assuming that the treaty was concluded on the faith of this declaration, the rights of an individual to his property cannot be affected by it.

So that, whether true or false, whether the declaration being made was a motive to the treaty—if it turned out in point of fact, that grants *were* made subsequent to the 13th of May, 1846, by which there became vested, either by actual or inchoate title, property in the lands of Mexico in a Mexican citizen, or in anybody else—the treaty could have no operation to

divest such rights; it being the universal principle of inter-
national law in this age of the world, that the cession of territory from one foreign Government to another, cedes only that
which the foreign Government has at the time of the cession.
No matter what general declarations were made. If erroneous
and false in point of fact, the rights of the individual are still
protected; and the Government deceived seeks an indemnity
from the Government deceiving.

The Court here took a recess.

—

ON RE-ASSEMBLING,

MR. RANDOLPH said—If your Honors please, Mr. Johnson
is kind enough to give me a few minutes of his time, on a
point entirely personal. I acknowledge myself very happy to
receive instruction from a gentleman of his eminence and
experience, whether given in a mode of advice or reproof.

Insomuch as concerned Mr. Benjamin, on Saturday last, I
supposed it was exceedingly manifest how I had labored for
the purpose of expressing how much I respected him personally and professionally, and at the same time to express how
little I respected or regarded so much of his argument as I felt
myself called upon to reply to.

I am sure that Mr. Johnson himself does not entertain a
higher regard for Mr. Benjamin *personally* than I do; and that
he cannot entertain so high a respect for him professionally,
because *I* am willing to admit him as a superior—which I
suppose *he* would not.

As to this simple matter of criticism of rhetoric, I think it
is unfitly qualified when it is called "unkind;" because the
thing is itself of a nature concerning which unkindness could
not be attached to the words used. I regarded that portion of
the matter as one of those lighter passages, which if unhap-
pily executed, at any rate would carry with it no semblance of
indignation, or malignity, or malice, or disrespect.

Mr. Benjamin—If your Honors please, I was not aware that I was on trial in the Court. Being so, I suppose I ought to say a word; to express the entire satisfaction with which I regard what has been said so justly by both gentlemen in my praise, and only to complain that they have not gone quite far enough.

Mr. Johnson—Some gentlemen are hard to satisfy, may it please your Honors. I can go no farther. I have gone far enough ; as far as my conscience will permit me.

It is due to myself, may it please your Honors, to speak seriously, to say in the presence of my brother on the other side, and in the hearing of the Bench, that I have said nothing in a spirit of unkindness to him. He has been uniformly so courteous and polite to *me*, that it would not be in my nature to utter a word of unkindness to *him*. In this room, and socially, I have had the pleasure of his company, and have enjoyed it, I am sure, as much as any friend he has. If, therefore, in the discussion and argument hereafter, in the excitement of the moment, I should drop an expression or utter language that may seem harsh, I hope he may understand it as explained in advance.

I was commenting, may it please your Honors, at the close of the first part of the session of the Court, upon the persevering determination of the Government not to permit the claimants in this case to have the benefit of the Mexican archives. They did not ask the Government to receive those archives as conclusive upon the questions at issue between ourselves and the Government. We knew, and were perfectly willing if it depended upon any assent of ours, that it would be in the power of the Government to deny the authenticity of those documents, the integrity of the archives, the honesty of the officers by whom they were preserved. But, in common with my colleagues, I think it especially unjust to us, and insulting to the Government of Mexico, to doubt the integrity of her archives, after what had occurred as between the two Governments, and what had from time to time been said in relation to the archives, by your Honors, or his Honor to whom I particularly address myself—the District Judge—before whom these questions have been, of course, presented, as well as the Supreme Court of the United States.

In the several decisions pronounced by his Honor, in the re-view of those decisions pronounced by the Supreme Court of the United States, in the various cases that have found their way before that tribunal—the evidence furnished by the archives has been considered conclusive practically, the one way or the other, if uncontradicted. A claim presented, not appearing in the Mexican archives, was, because of that fact, considered to be almost conclusively defeated. A claim presented, and opposed by the Government upon the ground of fraud, was considered to be almost conclusively established by the fact that the title to the claim was to be found in the archives. And the United States, whose officers could not really have supposed, had no right to suppose, and could not have supposed that the archives of Mexico were fraudulently made up, for in various cases, and particularly in one which they were very anxious to establish as fraudulent, and to defeat because fraudulent, availing themselves of the comity due by Mexico to themselves, they have asked through the Minister of the United States, for the time being, in the City of Mexico, the privilege of having examined the archives for the purpose of using it on the part of the United States to defeat the particular claim to which I now advert. I mean the claim of Limantour. And his Honor Mr. Justice Hoffman, in the very able opinion pronounced by him in that case, in his very clear and satisfactory presentation of all the evidence by which he was induced to come to the conclusion that the claim was fraudulent—a conclusion to which he leads the mind of his reader by a process of reasoning amounting almost to demonstration—relies upon the *absence* of the title in the archives, as conclusive evidence against the validity of the claim. And how did the evidence furnished by those archives, get here, may it please your Honors? I read from page 45 of the pamphlet copy of the opinion which his Honor was kind enough to give me a few days ago, in which he says:

On the Limantour and Castañares petitions the impression of

the type is not shown upon the last page of the paper. On all the other papers this impression is visible on all the pages of each sheet, indicating that the sheet must have been folded when placed under the press. These coincidences, though affording of themselves no conclusive evidence of the spuriousness of these titles, are yet significant as corroborating and confirming our conclusions drawn from other testimony, and as showing that every circumstance connected with them, even the most minute, points unmistakably in the same direction.

Such is the result of the rigorous and thorough examination which has been made of the archives of this Department.

That reference is to the archives here in California. The opinion then continues; and it is to this portion that I invite the attention of the Court:

It is shown that the archives at the City of Mexico are equally silent as to the alleged concessions or confirmations in these cases. It appears, that on the 4th of March, 1854, Mr. Cripps, the American Chargé d'Affaires at that city, addressed an official note to Bonilla, the Mexican Minister of Exterior Relations, requesting to be informed whether any record or evidence of titles granted to José Y. Limantour existed in the archives of Mexico. To this note Bonilla replies by inclosing to Mr. Cripps communications received by himself from the Heads of the Departments, to whom he had applied for the information required.

The same *Departments* to which we *now* refer; the same Heads of Departments on which we *now* ask your Honors to rely.

The opinion then proceeds to give the substance of the replies of each one of these Heads of Departments, in which each one states that the archives of his department have been examined, and that they contain no evidence whatever of the alleged grants to Limantour!

Your Honor then goes on to say:

The communication from the Minister of War and Marine, and from that of the General and Public Archives of the Nation, are to the same effect; and in the communication of the Minister of Foreign Affairs to Mr. Cripps, of the 6th December, 1855, he informs the latter that the three offices, of Fomento, of War, and of the General Archives, are the only ones where the evidences of the alleged grants could be found in the City of Mexico. He therefore refers Mr. Cripps to the archives of the public offices of California. How unproductive the search in these latter has been, we have already seen.

No doubt there, when it served the purposes of the United States, of the integrity of those archives? No intimation *there* that it was possible that the heads of the several departments in which these archives were found, were capable of "forgery, fabrication, fraud, falsehood, antedating!"

On the contrary, the United States relying, as your Honor justly relied, on the integrity of these very archives, was, by means of these very archives, decided to own the lands covered by the claim of Limantour.

Let *us*, then, have justice. Do not appeal to Mexico to save the United States from grants alleged to have been fraudulently concocted, by giving the United States the benefit of the evidence of the fraud furnished by the archives; and when a claimant in another case challenges the production of the same evidence, deny it upon the ground that "*We* say fraud existed, and we will not permit *you* to say the contrary by proof which in another case we not only *relied* upon, but insisted was *conclusive.*"

Now, what are those archives, may it please your Honors? Why, there are five of them; five of them in which is to be found evidence for or against the validity of the particular titles which we are now examining:

First. The espediente from the *Junta de Fomento;* now called the *Administration del Fundo.*

Second. The espediente from the Ministry of Justice; now in the Ministry of Relations.

Third. From the Ministry of Relations, Government and Police; now in the Ministry of *Gobernacion.*

Fourth. Another from the *Junta Facultativa* of the National College of Mining, which bears the same name at present.

Fifth. Another from the archives of the Direction of said College; bearing the same designation at present.

Some of these Superintendents of the Archives are the same men, if not *all* the identical men, who superintended the archives in which the evidence referred to in Limantour's case were kept.

Now what has to be done in order to make a forgery in any particular title effective? Corrupt one? No. Corrupt the officers in five departments. You might go to Washington —and I state it only as a bare possibility, not any time applicable to the heads of the several Departments—and it is barely possible under the state of things which has been existing for the last fifteen or twenty years, a change of subordinate officers being frequently made at the demand of active and noisy politicians during the immediately preceding Presidential canvass, that some dishonest man in some subordinate capacity might be found in some of the departments who might be open to corruption.

But, who has ever heard of any corruption in the head of a department? Who has ever heard of a bill of impeachment being shown up in Congress to secure the trial before the Senate of any of our Cabinet officers, suspected even on reasonable grounds of having violated the oath of their office and dishonored the Government and their own name?

Who has ever heard of any fraud being consummated against the United States through the instrumentality of corruption in any of our several Departments. We are as good, thank God, but we are no better than they are. The time has not yet come, and I trust in God it never will come, not only when any high officer of the Government has been corrupted, but when any man has ventured to approach such a personage with any offer to corrupt him. I disparage them not by comparing them with the officials who presided over the several Departments in Mexico, to which we have alluded. Read the testimony of these witnesses upon which my friend (Randolph) on the other side has commented. Read the searching examination through which he conducted them. See the ingenuity he displayed. Then answer for yourselves as to the results.

Great as brother Randolph's ingenuity is, versed as he was in the necessities of the particular case, anxious as he was to try the mental and moral calibre of these witnesses, we will submit to your Honors if it is not evident that, high as brother

Randolph's mental and moral qualities are—and nobody esti-
mates them higher than I do—he found his match in both of
these characteristics in the Mexican witnesses. Go to the testimony of Mr. Bassoco. See who got the best of it! Look to
his hypothetical questions, intended to dive into the mind of
the witnesses. Compare the answer with the question. The
"old man"—brother Randolph calls him *old*—he is younger
than I am, and I am not so very old; though I'm quite old
enough—he answers very kindly to one of my brother's inquiries, one of his hypothetical questions, and he answered in
Spanish. I did not know exactly what the phrase meant. I
asked, what does it mean? "*Quien sabe*" was the reply;
meaning, "who knows." "That is a foolish question."

Mr. RANDOLPH—That's the same phrase you translated
"Queen of Sheba," this morning.

Mr. JOHNSON—It admits of a great many translations; and
amongst others my brother will recollect that it means, "That's
a foolish question." I do not myself mean to apply the term
to any questions my brother Randolph may ask, but really I
do think, considering the relation in which the question was
put, that it was not altogether pertinent.

But, may it please your Honors, what right has any gentleman in a Court of Justice, and, above all, an officer of the
Government of the United States, *pro hæc vice*—what right has
he to charge witnesses with perjury and falsehood, when there
is no evidence upon the question of gentlemanly character,
when there is nothing in the evidence that does not show that,
to the best of their knowledge, they are telling the truth.

But there is said to be in their evidence enough to satisfy
us that they are *not* telling the truth. What is that? Why,
one man, Lanzas, did not know who his predecessor was, and
who his successor is. Well, there are a good many statesmen
in the United States who would be puzzled to give the like
information for themselves or for others. I think we can tell
who the successor of one of our high officials will be—just at
this speaking I think we can tell that.

Well, what is there of intrinsic evidence to be found in the record from the examination of these witnesses, that is calculated to satisfy your Honors that they are not telling the truth? Why, it is because they just repeated the lessons taught them before they came on to California! They knew exactly what was wanted. The case before they came here had got up to a certain point. It would not do. We were afraid, at least—so it is represented—that it would not do. We had what would have satisfied most minds that this title was perfectly fair. We had what we supposed ought to be received, so far as the Government was concerned, as evidence of the integrity of this title. We had the papers all authenticated by the officials of Mexico in the only way in which they could be authenticated; but the Government would not let it come in. Mr. Attorney General says: "I make it, of course, a matter of conscience and of principle not to let any evidence in that is going to hurt the United States." Then, what does my brother say? "Go to the City of Mexico, bring your nine witnesses here, and pay them two hundred thousand dollars for coming." We send to Mexico. William F. Barron went to Mexico. William E. Barron, "the simpleton," went to Mexico to get this testimony. He prepared it all when he got there, brought it up already made when he returned from there.

How did he go? My brother here upon my right (of course), who the counsel for the United States has not only not impeached, but on the uttering of a remark by me a few days ago intimated that the possibility of brother Randolph's involving *him* in the evil suppositions—from the instinct of his nature he said: "No; we make no charge against Mr. Billings;"—he accompanied Mr. Barron. He (Mr. Billings) is acknowledged to be incapable of falsehood or forgery. Not so, brother Billings, the thing was done, and *you* did it! You did it, if it was done at all. I have no idea that you shall escape at the cost of William E. Barron. He may be bad enough, but you are a great deal worse. *You* are no "*simpleton.*"

I speak of what is in the case, may it please your Honors; I am not going out of the record.

William E. Barron goes to Mexico, taking along with him as

counsel, Mr. Frederick Billings. They arrive there in the month of January; they stay there until the month of April. He (Billings) searched the archives. William E. Barron had no more to do with it than I had. He had too much sense —" simpleton" as he may be and is called by the special counsel —to interfere with it. He had with him a friend and counsellor who was competent to the work. He gets *him* there at considerable expense, no doubt, for he did not go without being paid, if he understands his profession—and from all that I can hear, he does—in that particular at least! He stays there three months. He worked like a mule. If there were any lessons taught to the Mexican witnesses, here is the master (patting Billings on the back). If there was any evidence prepared for the Mexican witnesses, here is the man who wrote it. If anybody corrupted the Mexican Minister, here is the man that in Mexico did it or advised it to be done!

MR. RANDOLPH—I do not agree with you in that.

MR. JOHNSON—I know you do not; but when you say that the fact is not so, we say that the charge is not so, and you thus give up the charge. I understand that you do not impute any such things to Mr. Billings, but in thus imputing it to no one, you should be logically and kindly consistent by saying that nobody did it; for, from the nature of the condition in which William E. Barron and Mr. Billings stood in the City of Mexico, it is impossible, if this was done at all by anybody, that it was not done by Frederick Billings—and nobody supposes that he did not. He would forfeit his life, if that were possible, fifty thousand times, rather than dishonor the name he has won for himself by so base an act of corruption and of treachery in an officer of this Court. *It was not done.* If done, brother Billings did it. But it was *not* done at all. It could *not* have been done, because, if contemplated, he was there to perform it.

Then, what was obtained there was all honestly obtained.

MR. RANDOLPH—We had copies of the papers before sent from there. We had already proof of their being there.

MR. JOHNSON. Copies? I am speaking now of archives, originals. You said the other day that we had "copies" in advance of their inquiry. You said that they would not do.

And, in addition to the proof that he got from Mexico, confirming the evidence that was here, he brought farther proof that was not here; he brought the archived entries of the actes.

I beg his (Billings) pardon for, even argumentatively, supposing that it was possible for him to have had anything to do with a transaction as infamous as this would have been, if it had occurred.

Then, what is the inference?

Suppose Limantour had said, when the United States received the evidence furnished by a certificate showing that his titles were *not* spread upon the Mexican archives, that the certificate was fraudulently obtained, forged, manufactured by the agent of the United States, the *Chargé d'Affairs*, or at his instigation? How indignant would everybody have been at such a charge! And that indignation, then, however high might be in point of fact the character of the representative of the United States at that time in Mexico, at whose instance these certificates were obtained, will be infinitely greater when you know who was the gentleman by whom *this* evidence was obtained, from a knowledge of him for years, as an officer of this Court, as a citizen, and as a man, and know that it is impossible that such falsehood could have been manufactured in the City of Mexico, and that witnesses could have been induced to come here for the purpose of making good the falsehood, you will be obliged to conclude that there was no falsehood about it. What the archives are said to prove the archives do prove.

Mr. Billings examined them. He is Spanish scholar enough not to be cheated. Looking not for falsehood, but for truth, carrying out the design that my brother (Benjamin), myself, and Mr. Crittenden, and Mr. Rockwell, had in making the several offers to the Government. We said: for Heaven's sake, in the name of justice and of mercy to these men, do let the archives themselves tell their honest story. If it shall turn out that they involve Castillero in the charge of fraud, which you impute to him or involve us, let the truth, whatever it may be, come out.

Mr. Billings was searching for the truth, with no fear, with no alarm, with no apprehension that his friend and his client would be involved injuriously by the search; but with that perfect confidence which he had from what he had seen before, that there was no ground whatever for the charge; he conducted the examination himself throughout; brings the witnesses here, examines the witnesses here, having had an opportunity of fully knowing the witnesses in Mexico; and yet, may it please your Honors, although he is not charged—if the charge is true, it especially involves him; he is practically charged with converting some Scotchman into *Castillo Lanzas*, and passing him off here as the former Secretary of Foreign Relations. His client is charged with it; but he stood by and saw it done! He must have known that *Castillo Lanzas* was either *the Lanzas*, or was an impostor.

My brother on the other side is not satisfied himself that he was *Castillo Lanzas*. He gave us an account the other day of his having tried to get at the fact through the instrumentality of a photograph. *Lanzas* was taken—photographically—and these vile photographs, as some of us know to our cost, always represent a man just as he is. Your Honors, perhaps, have found that out. I dread one of them a great deal more than I do a Mexican official!

Well, that is sent on. He sent it. It was a true likeness, you know. It was Lanzas who was photographed, whoever he was. It goes on to the District Attorney of *the United States*, at Washington, and he has not been able to get an answer as to who *Lanzas* was. But still he (Randolph) insists upon it that he may be, after all, only a school-master and a Scotchman.

MR. RANDOLPH (interrupting)—He may be a butler.

MR. JOHNSON—Yes, anybody but *Lanzas*. It is not in the scope of probability that he is *Lanzas!*

MR. RANDOLPH—That is not what I said.

MR. JOHNSON—Then it is *possible* that he *is* Lanzas? If

"possible" then, I think that the Court will come to the conclusion that it was Lanzas himself!

These gentlemen being here, what right has my brother on the other side to charge them all with being perjurers. Their testimony is not called in doubt by anything on the face of the record. The question is so plain, as a matter of evidence, that it would be doing injustice to the Court to take up any more time in discussing it.

Then you are to believe that these men told the truth.

Now, start with that idea, if your Honors please. Telling the truth, meaning to tell the truth, could they have been honestly mistaken? Why, certainly not. What are the facts that they testify to? The condition of the archives. They had just seen them. They had taken notes in order to enable them to testify. They were perfectly conversant with the points to which they did testify.

Mistake was impossible; perjury was out of the question. All that is left, is what we want—the truth.

Assuming as true what they have testified to be true, provided the papers found in the archives constitute the title of the mine and the two leagues, the case of the Government is at an end. It is not a hostile claim made up by force of false title papers; it is an honest claim which the United States, under the circumstances in which the case stands now, should almost blush to oppose.

The law upon the matter presents quite a distinct inquiry.

One of my colleagues has prepared for me a reference to the record, in which your Honors will find the pages given in which each one of these archives is proved, and the manner by which the proof was made. In some instances, they prove each other.

The particular title paper which appears in one bureau, appears in the same form with some additional matter in another. The short minutes of these several bureaus, which appear in some one bureau, are to be found in another. The witnesses speak of the fact of their being there.

If it were possible, as the case stands, to doubt the integrity of that proof, how would it be possible judicially to doubt it in a case in which the United States is a party, with every means to procure the evidence to establish the fraud, and not only not taking it, as we are told, but not venturing to take it upon the idle and unjust pretense that the Mexican officials are dishonest!

The grant for two leagues is dated on the 23d of May, 1846. I have compared, with the aid of Mr. Hopkins, the signature to that grant, which is the one we produce, and which we say is *Castillo Lanzas'* signature, with a signature to a grant made in the preceding month of March, in a communication.

MR. RANDOLPH—Do you propose to put Mr. Hopkins on the stand?

MR. JOHNSON—No; I propose to put the *book* on the stand, and to let the *book* speak for itself.

Mr. Hopkins has told us what he thought your Honors will see by inspecting the archives, that the signatures are identical. And you will see by looking at the same book of archives, that the paper which was used in 1846, on the 23d of May, is precisely the same paper that was used in January, 1846, up to that time, and differs from the paper which was used in 1845.

MR. RANDOLPH—(with Mr. Johnson's permission): It seems to me that this is some new evidence, which the gentlemen, I suppose, intend to rely upon, of which I have neither had notice nor opportunity for cross-examination, nor privilege to do or say anything at all in regard to. The instant Mr. Hopkins produced these books I availed myself of the moment to object to them; or to anything of that sort being introduced in this stage of the case. I am at a loss to know by what means they expect to establish the propositions they are now advancing by anything legitimately in the record of this case. I suppose they could only be established by the examination of Mr. Hopkins.

MR. JOHNSON—I don't propose to examine Mr. Hopkins; but your Honors will see, by looking at the record, that my friend (Mr. Randolph) himself examined Castillo Lanzas as to these very archives.

MR. RANDOLPH—If they are in the record I do not object to your using them.

MR. JOHNSON—Of course the originals are not in the record, but the signatures are copied. You cannot tell the character of a signature by a printed record. The originals in the records are extracts, not traced copies. My brother Randolph examined Lanzas in relation to them, and therefore made them evidence so far that your Honors are bound to go into the examination of the originals.

MR. RANDOLPH—The record must speak for itself on these points, and so far as they are concerned the Court will not depart from its rule of strictly confining its examination to the record.

MR. JOHNSON—Then the proposition, as I understand it, is that your Honors are not at liberty to look at the papers in the archives. I am taking the ground, that if you have any doubt about these signatures, you have the right to go to the archives and compare signatures. I do not want you to consult the archives unless you are in doubt; but if you doubt the integrity of the signature, compare it with the archives in the possession of the United States, and compare the paper used at this very time when the particular grant which we now offer in evidence was made, with that used in 1846.

And is there anything but the archives, may it please your Honors? Why, if we had no other proof than was furnished by the report of Lafragua, to which you have had a reference, it would be sufficient for this purpose.

MR. JUSTICE HOFFMAN—Do you mean to say that we cannot examine any original papers (addressing Mr. Randolph)?

MR. RANDOLPH—I mean to say, that I do not know what paper they intend to use which is not in this record. I do not know that the paper produced now will agree with the paper produced in the record. Nobody has more confidence in Mr. Hopkins than I have. But what I now object to is, the bringing in of matter as evidence now which might have been brought out when he was on the stand.

MR. JUSTICE HOFFMAN—Of course the introduction of new evidence now is objectionable. But what I want to know is, whether you object to originals or any other paper being introduced ?

MR. RANDOLPH—I understand that certain papers are now for the first time to be introduced before the Court. In order to identify these papers as coming from the archives of this State, Mr. Hopkins must be sworn. I do not desire to consent to any new examination of any description.

MR. JUSTICE HOFFMAN—I do not understand that to be the matter at issue at all.

MR. RANDOLPH—I do not presume to say how your Honors will judicially determine this matter. That is altogether for yourselves to decide.

MR. JOHNSON—I am not about to examine Mr. Hopkins. Mr. Hopkins has been examined. I am about to appeal, when the paper comes in, to induce your Honors to examine it for yourselves. When we are disputing about the integrity of a particular paper, upon the ground that it has not the signature of the man by whom it purports to have been signed, not only is it evidence, but the best evidence in the world is the production of the original paper. You cannot tell, by this printed record of the character, the similarity of a signature.

If you will turn to page 2373 of the Transcript, your Honors will find some of the questions propounded by Mr. Randolph. He propounded *several*, I should judge, from the fact that the one I commenced reading from, is numbered "738." I think that brother Randolph beat brother Peachy on that score—and that was pretty hard work.

Q. 738. Have you any recollection of having transmitted to the Governor of California any communication other than the dispatch concerning a grant of land to Andres Castillero ?
A. Not a distinct recollection of any particular communication, but the circulars which were sent to the other Governors were transmitted to him likewise.
Q. 739. Look at the writings to be found on pages 273, 274,

275, 276 and 277 (in red ink), in volume 18, from the office of
the Surveyor-General of California, and indorsed "Decrees and
Dispatches, 1845 and 1846," and say whether the circular dated
January 14th, 1846, and the decree dated March 13th, 1846,
and the circular dated March 24th, 1846 (copies of which are
herewith filed and marked respectively, "Exhibits Castillo
Lanzas Nos. 345, W. H. C."), respectively bear your genuine
signature?

A. They do bear my genuine official signature.

Q. 740. What is the difference between your official signature and your private signature?

A. In my private signature I write my full name, and in the
official signature, as Secretary of State, only one-half of the
name is generally written, as I stated the other day.

Q. 741. On these papers I observe that you write your name
"Castillo Lanzas," and that your signature as you write it in
signing the direct examination is "Castillo y Lanzas;" what is
the reason of the difference—is it casual, accidental, or is there
any reason for it?

A. It is because my half-signature has been, invariably,
"Castillo Lanzas," in which I always omit the Christian names,
the "de" and "y."

[Counsel for the United States offers in evidence copies of the
documents, with translation, referred to in question 739.]

This is the paper, the original of which we wish to present.
When the question is whether the originals are what they
purport to be, and that depends upon the evidence furnished
by the originals themselves, when the handwriting is disputed
and the signature is disputed, indisputably is it the best way
to produce the originals and then decide the question.

MR. RANDOLPH—That paper does not contain his official
signature.

MR. JOHNSON—No. He (Randolph) says that it is not
Lanzas' official, but his private signature, which is here given.
So much the better for him.

I pass on until Mr. Hopkins comes in. Then your Honors
will decide this matter for yourselves. All that I say now is,
that an inspection of the original book in which Mr. Secretary
Lanzas says is to be found his genuine signature, corresponds

exactly, both as to paper and as to signatures, with the paper upon which our grant is written, with the signature attached to that grant, and which Lanzas at the Bar has sworn was his.

MR. BILLINGS—(Interrupting.) Mr. Hopkins is out of town, and will not be in until morning.

MR. JOHNSON—I am very unwilling to ask for an adjournment sooner than the usual hour; but I am very weary, and if the Court will oblige me by an adjournment until morning, I shall consider myself as receiving a favor at their hands.

[The Court adjourned until morning.]

SECOND DAY.

SATURDAY, November 3, 1860.

MR. JOHNSON—I do not propose, may it please the Court, to add anything farther to satisfy you of the authenticity of the Mexican archives, or the claim to credit of the witnesses who came from Mexico and here testified to the integrity of those archives. I shall assume, or might assume, that the character of those archives could not be questioned by any one; and all that I propose to say in addition now is, that, supposing it to be barely possible that your Honors might call in question the authenticity of the archives, and the fact that they disclose the title under which our clients claim, that doubt may be removed by the evidence outside of the archives, not derived at all from the witnesses by whom the archives have been proved.

The evidence to which I refer is, in part, found in Mr. Lafragua's report. I hold in my hand what purports to be an authenticated copy of that report, printed by order of the Mexican Government. Beside this copy—which was produced and positively authenticated by Mr. Bassoco, one of the Mexican witnesses, as your Honors are aware—another copy has been offered in evidence, which at one time came into the possession of my colleague (Mr. Benjamin) who is immediately next to me, and which has been by him established, as far as his means of establishing it goes.

My brother upon the other side seemed to suppose—not that in point of fact there was any evidence which would lead, looking to the book itself, any intelligent man to the conclusion that this report had been fabricated in whole or in part—and has told your Honors, that it was "barely possible" that such a thing may have been done.

Now, even assuming the existence of that "bare possibility," I am sure I need not say to the Court that that is no ground upon which a judicial judgment can be placed. You are to decide upon *probabilities*, and not upon *possibilities ;* and if, in deciding between the probability and the possibility, you come to the conclusion that the probability infinitely outweighs the possibility, you will rest your judgment upon the probability.

But what is the supposed possibility, even if you could look to that for the purpose of guiding you in your conclusions as to the fact? What is the ground of that possibility? This book purports to be an official publication ; a report by an official—a fact conceded at the time—to his Government, and published by the authority of the Government. It is published in Mexico. Nobody can question that. It is published in Mexico, on or about the time when it purports to have been published. Nobody can well question that ; and it contains not only a reference to the mine which is in dispute in this case, but it contains also an account of all the transactions in which that Government, during the period covered by the report, had been engaged, which fell within the jurisdiction of this particular officer. It is such a report of the proceedings of his particular department to his Government, during the period embraced by the report, as is the report of any of our Secretaries to the President, and communicated by the President to Congress ; made to the President for the purpose of being communicated to Congress, and published by the authority of Congress.

My brother has thought that he might with great propriety challenge your Honors' assent to the authenticity of the papers to which he has referred ; that he might with great propriety refer to the documentary proceedings of Congress ; that he could refer with propriety, and ask you to concede, with him, that there was no doubt of the fact to which he referred to the publication of speeches in the *Congressional Globe.* He has referred you to a speech made by Col. Benton, in 1850, two years after the treaty between Mexico and the United States was negotiated, for the purpose of satisfying your Honors why it was that the 10th Article in the original *projet* of the treaty had been stricken out by the Senate. Suppose we were to say, what proof, Mr. Randolph, have you to satisfy the Court that the Executive Document No. 17, is what it purports to be, and was published at the time when it seems to have been published?

4

What proof have you that the *Congressional Globe* is *the Congressional Globe*, and was published at the time when it prefaces to be published ? Catching the suspicion which floats in the mind of my friend on the other side, and has been floating there since the commencement of this discussion, I almost begin to think it was contagious—the moment he put the book down, by an effort of instinct which I could not help, I took up the copy of the *Globe* that he had referred to, looked at the leaves in every form in which I thought it was possible to discover whether those leaves had been incorporated into the report, went through the same process with the Executive Document—and I was almost inclined to believe that my friend on the other side, or the United States, had actually forged and manufactured that report.

I have great respect, as I am sure your Honors have, and all who know him, for his intellect, and for his knowledge ; and when he said so positively, and in conducting the examination in relation to the authenticity of this report seemed to be so convinced, that those leaves upon which we were relying were interpolated into this report, and made long after the period when, according to this report, the report itself seems to have been published, I began to think that there was no reliance to be put upon anything. And indeed he, I think, on the second day of his argument, or the first—told the Court that it was almost impossible to arrive at certainty about anything. He did not know absolutely whether he had come from his house that morning and was here at all. I do not know whether he doubted his being here. *We* did not doubt it. *We* heard him, and *we* recognized his voice. *We* never shall forget it.

" There is no matter !" said one of the philosophers ; " man is not sensitive, and man does not exist !" Dr. Johnson suggested a very sensible way to satisfy him that he had some feeling. " Try his shin with a club, and see if he does not cry out !"

There are some things, may it please your Honors, about which the human judgment has no right to doubt ; and one of those is a publication made by a Government officer apparently for Government purposes, to accomplish some political policy of the Government of which the officer is a member. *That* is entitled to credit; and another thing is to be inferred as a matter of comity : that everything contained in the report made by such public officer is to be taken as true, as far as *motive* is concerned, as far as the determination to tell the truth is involved. The officer may be mistaken ; his judgment may be erroneous ; his memory may fail him ; but his *integrity* no man has a right to question, unless that integrity has been impugned by some evidence outside of the official paper in relation to which the question may arise. But Mr. Lafragua has been examined, and he tells you that this report is precisely what it appears to be; that it was published exactly as it purports to have been published ; that it was prepared by him in his official character, and in the discharge of his official duty.

MR. RANDOLPH—Mr. Lafragua did not testify to the volume at all. We had only a few pages presented by him.

MR. JOHNSON—All that relates to this matter was presented. He did not bring the whole book; but the whole book is here now. The whole book is here now for inspection. Both are here. When he (Lafragua) spoke of the authenticity of the particular extracts, he looked to the book to see if the extracts were in the book, or correctly taken from it. He took them out of the book, and swearing they were correctly taken out of the book, he necessarily testified to the existence of the book. He said he made the report. On page 18 of Transcript he says :

I made these marginal notes and annotations myself, to show what portions of the document relate to this particular subject. This document is taken out of a large bound volume which embraced my whole report as Minister of Relations, upon all subjects pertaining to my office, with accompanying documents. I took this portion for convenience, because it embraced everything which my said report contained relating to said Almaden mine, or Castillero's connection therewith.

My brother Benjamin, some time in 1848 or 1849, became the counsel of what is called the " Tehuantepec Company ;" a company the purpose of which your Honors are aware of. The success of that company depended, in part, on their being able to establish the validity of what was called the "Garay Grant." American citizens were invited to participate in the enterprise. The success of the enterprise would depend, more or less, upon the patronage extended to it by the Government. The company selected my brother as their counsel, for the purpose of enlightening, first, the public mind, and present the claim of that particular grant; and, secondly, for the purpose of instructing the Government as to the validity of the grant, in order to be able to obtain thereafter such assistance from the Government as the legitimate patronage of the Government might enable it to bestow.

And he is in search of information. With his usual industry he looks everywhere for sources of information. Mr. Garay himself is in Mobile, Alabama. He has come from Mexico. He meets him at Mobile for the very purpose of consulting upon the enterprise in which our citizens were about to engage, and in which Mr. Garay had an interest; and in the City of Mobile he is furnished by Mr. Garay with an exact duplicate, in all respects, of this document (Lafragua report).

What did Mr. Garay give it to him for? He was not at the time the counsel for the New Almaden Company, and had no idea of it! I do not know that he *knew* of the existence of the New Almaden mine, except as a general historical matter of which he may have become acquainted from the newspapers of the day. Mr. Garay gave it to him for the purpose of informing him and enabling him to set the public mind right on the validity of the Garay grant; and the validity of that grant depended upon acts of the Mexican Government. Here was an official report made by an officer before whom, in the discharge of his official duty, the existence and the validity of that grant would have appeared.

He (Mr. Benjamin) marks the passages in the book which relate to the Garay grant. He looked no farther. He searched, and Garay re-searched, for the purpose *exclusively* of obtaining information in relation to that grant. And the report that he made, and the speech that he made to the citizens of Louisiana to induce them to enter into this enterprise, was a report or speech made in part from the information obtained by him out of this document—as he tells us in his testimony.

MR. RANDOLPH—Please refer to that testimony.

MR. JOHNSON—Your Honors have, I believe, a copy of the Transcript before you. Mr. Benjamin's testimony is to be found on page 3026 of the Transcript: " State your name, age and residence."

MR. BENJAMIN—Don't read the age.

MR. JOHNSON—No, I will not read the age; but as you first put it, it is lawful age. Well, everybody believed *that*. I will skip the rest; but that tells more against my brother than if I was to read it. Take the next question :

Examine *Exhibit Bassoco No. 3, O. H.* on file in this case, purporting to be a printed copy of the report of Lafragua, Minister of Relations, to the Mexican Congress, etc.

This is the document that had been proved by Mr. Lafragua, and by Mr. Bassoco, too. The question is :

Examine *this document* (which I now hold in my hand) on file in this case, etc., and state if you have a duplicate of said Exhibit; and if you have, please produce it, and state when it first came into your possession, under what circumstances you received it, and from whom, etc.

This is the one he examined (holding up a volume). He said he got this in 1849; that he examined it, and upon comparing it with the one proven by Lafragua and Bassoco, and marked Bassoco No. 3, he finds that his is a duplicate of the other "which had been forwarded from the City of Mexico to Don José Garay, and was by him delivered to me. It was furnished me for the purpose of proving the legality and validity of that (the Garay) grant, about which doubts had been raised in the United States. I was chairman of a sub-committee of the citizens of New Orleans, who had held a public meeting for the purpose of devising means of securing possession of that grant," etc. "I received at the same time from Mr. Garay a number of other pamphlets and books in reference to the Tehuantepec grant."

Well, I will stop there. I suppose nobody could doubt from that general comparison, that this (the one that was before filed) is an exact counterpart of the one produced by my brother. But the evidence shows that the portions of the two reports involved in this case, were compared together by my brother upon the other side, and Mr. Benjamin, and found to his (Mr. Randolph's) satisfaction to be identical, word for word. Indulging in the suspicion, which is a part of his nature as far as this case is concerned—and which has almost got to be a part of my own, for I have caught it—my brother seemed to suppose that by some hocus-pocus or other these extracts which appear upon the record of this New Almaden mine controversy, got into the copy produced by my brother Benjamin, not through any instrumentality of *his,* but by means of contrivances set on foot by somebody else; and he goes upon the search in this wise—I mean in search for the just foundation of his suspicion :

What did you do with the book after you had used it for the purpose for which you obtained it from Mr. Garay ?
I had it in New Orleans.
Had anybody any access to it ?
No, not as far as I know.
What did you do with it afterwards?
Why, having to use the information it contained, and it being my voucher for the truth of the representations I made in relation to the Garay grant, I brought it with me in my trunk to Washington.
What did you do with it then ? Where did you keep it ?
I kept it in my room in my lodgings at Washington.
Up stairs, or down ?
Up; next to my library, in my office.
Where did you keep it ?
In the next room.
In your office, in a book-case ?
Yes.
Was there a key to it ?
Yes.
Did you lock it ?
No.

Then, he was satisfied; the thing was out; my brother's suspicion turned out to be particularly well-founded! Not even suspecting his suspicion, my brother Benjamin had indifferently said that he had handed the book to a Mr. John A. Rockwell. " Well, and why?" " He came to see me about the Almaden case; I had received a letter from the agents of the Almaden Company in New York advising me before I saw Mr. Rockwell, that Rockwell would call upon me for the purpose of retaining my services in the Almaden case; and in the course of the interview between Mr. Rockwell and myself in relation to the Almaden case, he (Rockwell) said that the charge of fraud in relation to the title papers upon which the claim to the mine rested, was as he thought disproved, wholly unfounded, from evidence to be found in a report made by the Minister of Interior and Exterior Relations, Lafragua, as far back as 1846 or 1847, giving information to his Government of the conduct of the Government in relation to this very mine in 1845."

Not a word had dropped from Mr. Rockwell intimating that he knew that Mr. Benjamin had this copy; not a word—nor could there—because he did not know it. At the moment that the suggestion was made that this paper, or a paper like this— a report by Lafragua of the conduct of the Mexican Government in 1845, made by him in his official character to the Government of Mexico, contained conclusive evidence of the integrity of the title to the Almaden mine—my brother said: "I have got Lafragua's report." I know nothing about its contents, as far as relates to the Almaden mine; but I must have a copy of the report to which you refer, and let us see what it is.

And he goes to his *unlocked* book-case. There he finds it notwithstanding it was *unlocked*. He takes it out, finds the very evidence to which Mr. Rockwell had reference as being contained in that report; and Mr. Rockwell asks him to let him take it, which of course he did.

Your Honors, both of you, I think, know who John A. Rockwell is. A member of Congress originally — a distinguished member for many years; and now not only one of the most distinguished members of the Bar of the Supreme

Court of the United States, but a man of the most unquestioned honor. *He* takes this book in Washington for the purpose of preserving it, and getting it so authenticated as, if possible, to remove all doubts from the mind of the Attorney General, who had caught this "suspicious" disease. He goes to the Mexican Minister to give him an authentic certificate, that this report *is* what it purports to be. He keeps it.

MR. RANDOLPH—Is that certificate in evidence?

MR. JOHNSON—I do not offer it as evidence. It is there. I only want to show what Mr. Rockwell did. Mr. Benjamin speaks for himself. Here is the certificate; it speaks for itself. What did Mr. Rockwell do?

Mr. Benjamin, when did you next see that report after you gave it to Mr. Rockwell?
Well, the next time I saw it afterwards was in Washington, Mr. Rockwell showed it to me with the certificate annexed to it; I did not see it again till I saw it in San Francisco. Mr. W. E. Barron told me in New York, last July, that Mr. Rockwell had given it to him to be returned to me.

He was asked further about the book. He did not know the book had come on. All he recollected was, that he had given it to Rockwell. He wanted it here, very naturally, and he asked of Wm. E. Barron, one of the parties in this case, and who was to go on with Mr. Benjamin and myself as a friend and a client—a friend as intimately as he is a client—and Barron tells him, "Rockwell gave me the book to which I suppose you refer."

MR. RANDOLPH—Read the testimony.

MR. JOHNSON—Well, I will read the testimony. I cannot make it as strong as the witness makes it. Page 3028. He (Benjamin) says:

When I reached New York, last July, on my way to California, Mr. William E. Barron, of whom I inquired what Mr. Rockwell had done with the volume, told me he had it in his trunk; that Mr. Rockwell had given it to him to be returned to me; and on arrival at San Francisco, Mr. Barron took it from his trunk and delivered it to me; and here it is (holding up the volume).

Now, says my brother, what do you know was done with that paper, from the time it was handed to Rockwell to the period when, in San Francisco, William E. Barron handed it to you? Why it is fourteen months—

MR. RANDOLPH—Eighteen.

MR. JOHNSON—Eighteen months; still more striking, telling, and suspicious! Why, what an infinite deal of forgery can be done in eighteen months! And, may it please your Honors, awake still to the idea, carried away by the delusion—if he will permit me to say so—under which he had been laboring with reference to the original report of Lafragua, he questions my brother, a witness, to know whether in his opinion it would not have been possible, even if this book was a genuine book in relation to other matters, published at the time when it prefaces to be published, published in good faith under the instructions of the officer by whom the report purports to have been made, to have extracted from the original publication so much of it as relates to the mine; or, if there was nothing in it relating to the mine, to have taken out some of the original leaves containing other matter, and substituted there instead other leaves containing what is there now in relation to the mine! And they go into a trial of skill, as to the possibility of doing it! Mr. Benjamin says, with great simplicity, that he is not so well acquainted with the art and skill of the forger, as to believe it is probable. He thinks it is improbable. Everybody must say it is improbable.

Well now, if improbable, this report being true, what doubt can there be of the authenticity of the Mexican archives of which I spoke yesterday, if it was possible to doubt on that subject at all, without the aid of the report. The report, manuscript report, is here; all written, I have no doubt, in Mexico by my brother Billings. *He* got it written there in Mexico.

But, may it please your Honors, passing by these circumstances which hardly seem to have weight enough to be worthy of serious remark—assuming now that the report is what it purports to have been, that it represents correctly the transactions which it does represent—what possible doubt can there be that there was, in 1846, a communication made to the Mexican Government by Castillero, in relation to the mine, and that all the proceedings stated in the report in relation to the action of the Mexican Government upon that application of Castillero, took place? If they did, there is an end of the controversy, as far as the authenticity of the papers is concerned. But that is not all. Let me refresh the Court's recollection as to the contents of the extracts proved by Mr. Benjamin, and proved by Lafragua; and correctly proved, as appears by the production of the copies themselves to which they each testified. I read from page 1212 of the Transcript:

Secretary's Office of the Junta de Fomento
y Administrativa of Mining.

Most Excellent Sir:—In compliance with your Excellency's superior order of the 3d inst., directing this Junta to give an account of the matter confided to its care since the epoch of its report in 1845, their present condition, with the object in view, in order to form the *Memoria* which should be presented to the general Congress of the nation, immediately on its installation, the Junta has the honor to submit to your Excellency a simple historical relation of the most important matters with which it has been occupied for the last two years, and their present situation, with the reflections and recommendations which it has deemed suitable for the better and more faithful performance of its duties. * * *

It was Lafragua's business to make a report such as this; and amongst other objects, embraced by his official duties in that particular, were the proceedings of the Junta during the period to be covered by the report. And applying to the Junta to get information from them to enable him to make the report, he receives from the Junta a communication which I have just read in part.

Now what more did they tell him?

The Junta, on the 21st of April last, sent to the professional

Board of the College some specimens of cinnabar which Don Tomas Ramon del Moral presented, in the name of Don Andres Castillero, a resident of Upper California, with a representation in which he asked for assistance to work a mine which he had discovered in the Mission of Santa Clara, known by the old Indians who got out of it vermilion to paint their bodies. The assay made by the Professor of Chemistry, of the ores in common, produced the extraordinary *ley* of thirty-five and a half per cent., which was communicated to the Government on the 5th of May, representing that Señor Castillero had been asked what assistance he required of the Junta.

The archives prove exactly that fact; that on the 5th of May he was asked—having made known to them before the discovery of the mine, and its having turned out to be a mine of extraordinary richness—to state what assistance he required to the Junta.

What do they say then?

That Señor Castillero presented his petition in due form, and it was very attentively examined by the Junta; he made his propositions, to which this (Junta) agreed, to wit, that there should then be delivered to him five thousand dollars in money, eight iron retorts of those which the Junta ordered to be made for their former examinations, and all the quicksilver flasks it has in the *negociacion* of Tasco.

That is true; because that is precisely the answer made by Castillero when he is asked what assistance he required. He wanted, he said, the $5000, the eight iron retorts, and all the quicksilver flasks that the Junta had in the *negociacion* of Tasco.

What else did he do?

Señor Castillero obligated himself on his part to repay said advance in quicksilver, at the rate of one hundred dollars a quintal, within six months from his leaving the port of Mazatlan.

That is in his answer, as now spread upon the archives before your Honors. What else? They go on to say that—

This agreement was approved by the Supreme Government on the 20th of the same month.

The archives tell the same story to the letter. What else?

Why was it not carried out? They show why it was not carried out.

This agreement was approved by the Supreme Government, on the 20th of the same month; but on account of the declaration (of war) made by the United States of the North, when he was going to receive the draft on Mazatlan, the ministry issued the order of September 19th of this year, directing the suspension of all payments of the branch of quicksilver except the support of the college and expenses of the office. * * *

That was true, too, as is proved by the archives.

Now here is another extract from another part of the report. It is not the Junta still speaking, but Lafragua communicating what they have told him to the Congress, by whom the whole matter was to be examined:

In Upper California, a mine (*criadero*) has been discovered whose *ley* surpasses that of the best mine known, that of Almaden, which does not produce more than thirteen per cent., while ours, by the assays made in the College of Mining of this Capital, exceeds thirty-five and a half per cent.

Now let us turn to what the Junta itself has further said on the same subject to the Minister:

* * * This is not the occasion to present together all the labors of the Junta to correspond to the high confidence with which the Government has honored it. A part of them are expressed in this note, and the others may be found in the memorials, reports, and multitude of communications which are in the office of this ministry. For the present it will merely assure what is shown in these documents, to wit, that the spirit of enterprise has been so stimulated that the quicksilver mines in the principal Departments of the Republic are being worked, both by companies and also by individuals; that in the Department of San Luis Potosi, the quicksilver extracted is in proportion to the silver reduced, so that no foreign quicksilver is required; that in Upper California, in the Presidio of Santa Rosa, there has been discovered by Señor Don Andres Castillero a great mine, the *leys* of which are truly surprising, since the result of the assays——

They had then been made. So the archives say, and so our witnesses swear.

—made in the College of Mining gives, as the common fruits, over thirty-five and a half per cent., while that of the best mine which is known, that of Almaden, does not exceed thirteen per cent., and finally, that, from all the data collected, it may be hoped, resting on a good foundation, that our mines of quicksilver are more than sufficient to supply all that is required for the reduction of our silver.

This grand national enterprise the Junta has not been able fully to carry out, because it has been deprived of one of its funds of one per cent. of the circulation of money, without substituting any other, and because of the remainder it could only dispose of one-third part, since the Government, in the deficiency of the treasury, has used the rest. This evil was increased to the lamentable extremity of leaving it (the Junta) without any, by the order of the 10th May last, which directed the suspension of all the payments which were made by the public treasury.

They then go on to add:

The sad results of such determinations the Junta will not stop to detail; they are manifest from what has already been here shown. *   *   *   *   *   *   *   *   *

The Junta has the honor to present to your Excellency its highest consideration, most distinguished esteem, and most profound respect.

God and Liberty.

Mexico, November 17th, 1846.

VICENTE SEGURA,
President.

The Secretary being occupied,

ISIDRO R. GONDRA, 1st Clerk.

Now, that is dated, may it please your Honors—and God and Liberty are called upon to witness it—November the 17th, 1846, and signed by Vicente Segura, President of the Junta. It is impossible, then, to doubt, if the archives were out of view:

First. That there was communicated to the Junta the discovery of the mine.

Second. That there were specimens of the ore of the mine transmitted to Mexico for the purpose of being assayed.

Third. That these specimens were assayed and showed the extraordinary *ley* of $35\frac{1}{2}$ per cent.

Fourth. That in consequence of this, on the 5th of May, Castillero was asked by the Junta what assistance he proposed should be granted him on the part of the Mexican Government; that he made the propositions referred to by the Junta; that they were accepted by the Junta, as far as they had the authority to accept; and only not carried out because in the struggle between themselves, a comparatively feeble nation, and the immense power of the United States, the Government of Mexico wisely thought, with a view to defend themselves against subjugation by the United States, that they would retain all moneys in the hands of their several bureaus, hazard everything, sacrifice everything, for the purpose of defending their territories against the invasion of the United States.

That, and that alone, prevented the agreement from being carried out; and it is perfectly consistent with the fact of the agreement. All that is necessary for us to show in this case, is the existence of the agreement; the fact that it was entered into, by which, between Castillero and the Junta, there was a contract made (depending for its ultimate execution, of course, on the action of the Mexican Government), by which Castillero was to become, as far as the laws and Government of Mexico were concerned, the owner in this mine of all that under the laws of Mexico could constitute an individual proprietorship of a mine.

Mr. RANDOLPH—Both orders are mentioned; that of the 10th of May, and that of the 19th of September.

Mr. JOHNSON—That of the 19th of September, suspended *all* payments.

Mr. RANDOLPH—By which of the orders was Castillero prevented from receiving this assistance?

Mr. JOHNSON—That of the 10th of May, as I understand it. It makes no difference. He was prevented anyway. Whether the 10th of May, or the 19th September, is of no consequence. The acts say the 10th of May; but it is hardly material whether it was the one date or the other. If we find that at any date the Mexican Government took steps that prevented the Junta carrying out this agreement with Castillero, it proves the existence of the agreement.

MR. RANDOLPH—The communication says: " But on account of the declaration (of war) made by the United States of the North, when he was going to receive the draft on Mazatlan, the Ministry issued the order of September 19th of that year."

MR. JOHNSON—That is a mistake of the papers. It is the 10th of May. The act shows that. Your Honors see, that on looking at page 1213 of the Transcript, which I have read before—

" This evil" they say, was increased to the lamentable extremity of leaving it (the Junta) without any, by the *order of the 10th of May last*, which directed the suspension of all the payments which were made by the public treasury.

If your Honors will turn to page 1775 of the Transcript, you will have an explanation as to the differences in these dates:

This Junta received yesterday, Sunday the 20th, the official communication which your Excellency is pleased to address to it of the 19th inst., transcribing that of his Excellency the Minister of Finance, of the same date, in which the Junta is informed that his Excellency the General-in-Chief, in exercise of the Supreme Executive power, had thought proper to decree, in view of the official note of date the 12th, that there be given to the fund established for the Encouragement of Quicksilver Mines, the destination to which it is directed in favor of public instruction, but that the great penury of the Treasury being so notorious, the Supreme Government requires that from the dotal fund a loan be made to it of twenty-five thousand dollars, with the understanding that the payment of the same shall be decreed as soon as possible.

That is dated the 21st of September, 1846.

The Court will have no difficulty in understanding it. I do not care whether we are right or wrong as to dates. It is hardly material, the one date or the other. You may take the one date, but it all goes to prove that, owing to some cause, all that had been done was not carried out. There is no pretense of mistake as to dates, so far as this mine is concerned. That is the way the subject was before them on or about the 5th of May, when representation was made to Castillero to make a proposition. The proposition was made and accepted, but not carried out.

On the 29th of May, 1846, (page 1697 of Transcript):

It was also resolved, in conformity with the report of the Controller's office, that twenty-five dollars be paid to the Notary, Calapiz, for proceedings in the instrument of agreement which had been made with Don Andres Castillero, to assist his quicksilver enterprise in the mine of Santa Clara, in Upper California, embraced in the official order for the suspension of all payments for this branch.

Now, that proves beyond all doubt, provided the entries be correct, that an agreement had been made between Castillero and the authorized representative of Mexico upon this subject; that it had been reduced to writing; that the cost of reducing it to writing was $25, and that this $25 was directed to be paid to the Notary for his having transferred into writing the agreement between the Junta and Castillero. That is, as your Honor's see, on the 29th of May, 1846.

It is perfectly clear, then, may it please your Honors, if we stop here, that the facts upon which we rely, occurred on the dates when we say they did occur. But it is said by my brother that there are some suspicious circumstances; that notwithstanding all this testimony of the Mexican witnesses, and the confirmatory evidence to be found in the Lafragua report, there are some circumstances calculated still to leave doubt as to whether everything contained in those archives could have occurred. And one is, that it seems, according to our statement, that a man by the name of Piña, sailed from Monterey in a brig called the Hannah.

Well, now, I do not understand my brother, in reply, seriously to contest the fact that the Hannah *did* go down; *did* carry somebody; and *did* arrive, on or about the time when we say she did arrive. He had obtained, or his client (Laurencel) had obtained a deposition of a Capt. Paty, which was intended to show that *he* took Piña down.

Mr. Randolph—The deposition was intended to show that he took *Castillero* down; and that in the year 1859, when the deposition was given, Piña had never figured in the case, nor, so far as I knew what was to turn up in the case, in anybody's contemplation, until the year 1859.

Mr. Johnson—Then you took the deposition to prove that the vessel did not go down. Captain Paty's evidence is relied on, at least for the purpose of showing now—whether that was the original purpose for which it was offered or not—that Piña went with Castillero in another vessel. *We* say he went in the Hannah. *We* say the Hannah left Monterey at the time we have stated, and arrived on or about the 1st of April at Mazatlan.

Now, amongst other things, may it please your Honors, short of the direct evidence which we offered in advance, applicable to the locality of Monterey from which the vessel went, in order to show that our statement was right and that she arrived at Mazatlan on or about the 1st of April, we produced and proved a letter dated "On board the U. S. ship Portsmouth, in the port of Mazatlan, April 1st, 1846," purporting to have been written by Mott, Talbot and Co. You will find it at page 3020 of the Transcript. I will not stop to consider the weight of the evidence which establishes the authenticity of that letter. The evidence is all one way. The letter is found here amongst the papers of Thomas O. Larkin, after his death. The letter is proved by those who have been accustomed to see the signature of professed writers.

Now, assuming the letter to have been proved, and assuming —as you cannot avoid doing—that it is true, what does it establish with relation to the Hannah? Did such a vessel leave Monterey? Did she carry communications from Castillero? Did she stop at Mazatlan? Did she have communications from Mr. Larkin, directed to Mazatlan? And when did she arrive at Mazatlan? This letter bears date the 1st of April. What does it tell us? It is written on board the ship, and the writer begins by saying:—"It has been hinted to us that this ship" (the Portsmouth) "is bound to Monterey," (from whence we say Mr. Larkin had written to them,) "and although the fact is doubtful, we avail ourselves of the chance to acknowledge the receipt of your much valued favors of the 2d, 4th and 5th ult.," etc. "Your letters have this moment reached us per 'Hannah,' and we are much obliged for their contents. You were correct in supposing that the destination of this vessel when she sailed from this, was not known to us. * * * * We are much obliged for the fruit, which, however, as the 'Hannah' has just anchored, we have not yet received."

Then he goes on to speak of California. My brother sys seriously: That letter cannot be genuine, for who ever heard of fruit being in Monterey in March, 1846, and being sent down to Mazatlan? Well, I suppose such is possible in the course of nature, according to what I have seen here. You put the seed in the ground——

MR. RANDOLPH (interrupting) — The course of nature is changed in different places.

MR. JOHNSON—Nature is apt to be pretty much the same the world over. She is not in the hands of politicians. She has a sovereignty of her own, about which there can be no dispute. You may call it "squatter sovereignty," or call it anything else; we cannot reach it, and thank God we cannot. If we could, we would turn the world "topsy-turvy" in a very short time. No fruits in California! Why, if you put, I am told, a peach-stone in the earth, it bears peaches in ten months! Everything grows here wonderfully. A high officer, a valiant officer of the navy—I won't mention his name because he is single—after I had been here but a few days, came up to the office where I was, and said: "Come down, Colonel, I want you to see a little girl a year and a half old. She is taller and larger every way than our own folks at home at sixteen." " Why, said I, that is wonderful!" "Come down with me to the market. I will show you a peach you cannot get into your hat. Upon my honor it is true." Well, I could not doubt an officer's honor!

Well, now, may it please your Honors, he does not say it was California fruit; he only says he sent *fruit.*

MR. RANDOLPH—I give it up, if a baby is fruit.

MR. JOHNSON—A baby *is* fruit, but I suppose not the fruit he sent down in jars.

Well, the fruit has gone there, and the vessel is there on the 1st of April. She goes there from Monterey, and she goes there bearing letters from Mr. Larkin. Well now, what have we done? Why, we have produced Mr. Larkin's books. These colleagues of ours, Messrs. Halleck, Peachy and Billings —and they have the means of doing it honestly—they are not satisfied with presenting a case for hearing until they have presented *all* the evidence that is to be procured anywhere. They wanted to prove amongst other things, that the Hannah *did* sail; and they produced a letter dated the 23d of April of that year to Capt. Gillespie from Mr. Larkin, and copies of letters written by Mr. Larkin, by the Hannah, in which he speaks of the Hannah. Not satisfied with that, they were successful in finding a species of blotter kept by Mr. Larkin as an official book in order to show the daily transactions at the Consulate, for the purpose of showing that there *was* a ship called the Hannah, where she came from to Monterey, when she arrived in Monterey, and where she went to from Monterey. Now, as to the last, first.

This looks a good deal like a genuine book (holding up a volume.) It is not only proved by Mr. Swasey—as *he* has *not* sworn that it *is* a genuine book, the probability is that it *is !* Young Mr. Larkin produces it; and *he* says that it is one of the books of his father. What is it? A strange sort of diary, kept day by day by the father, as you see. All sorts of things in it; transactions of the household, as well as transactions of the Consulate.

Under date of February, 1846—the date is at the head of the folio from which I now read—he says :

Thursday, 12—Brig Hannah, from Mazatlan.

Where was she at the time of this entry? In Monterey. How long did she stay? And when she went off, where was she destined? Let the book answer again.

Under the head of March, 1846—again I read from the head of the page—he says:

Saturday, 7—Brig Hannah, for Mazatlan.

Now, if these entries are genuine—and nobody questions it—she arrived here *from* Mazatlan on the 12th of February; and she left here *for* Mazatlan, on the 7th of March, 1846.

MR. RANDOLPH—You proved she went to San Blas first.

MR. JOHNSON—I do not care where she went. She may have gone around the globe, or to the Indies; it is perfectly immaterial. I have got her here "for Mazatlan." The entry in the Consul's book says she was destined "for Mazatlan." That she *was* destined for Mazatlan is certain; that she *got to* Mazatlan on the first of April is equally certain—for that is proven by Mott, Talbot & Co's letter.

Now, what did she carry? Turn to page 2667 of the Transcript. You will find what is proved to be a correct copy from an original letter taken from the Consular book, dated "Consulate of the United States—Monterey, California, March 8th, 1846," directed to Colonel Fremont:

SIR:—With this you have my Consular answer to the General and Prefecto's to you of last week, etc. * * * * By your messenger of last week I forward some United States newspapers, etc. * * * * I then informed you that there was an American brig (brig "Hannah") of Salem, at anchor in this port, *bound to Mazatlan*, whose supercargo I had requested to remain here until the third day, to enable you to send letters to the United States, if you were so inclined.

Now, I assume that letter to be what it purports to be—an authentic letter; nobody can doubt it. And Mr. Larkin told the truth when he communicated, antecedent to the 8th of March, to Col. Fremont, by letter, that there was in Monterey a vessel called the *Hannah;* that she was about to leave upon or before the fifth; that he had persuaded her supercargo to remain until the third day, to enable Fremont, by her, to inform the Government of the United States of the transactions in

California, provided he should think proper to transmit any communication.

But that is not all. On the 3d of April, 1846, there is another letter, dated the 3d of April, port of Monterey—and is to be found on page 2667 of Transcript:

CONSULATE OF THE UNITED STATES OF AMERICA, }
Port of Monterey, Cal., April 3d, 1846. }

SIR:—Don Andres Castillero, formerly member of Congress from this Department, leaves this port in a few days for Acapulco, on board the Hawaiian barque *Don Quixote*, as Commissioner to Mexico, from General José Castro, Military Comandante of California; he will arrive in Mexico by the twenty-fifth or thirtieth of this month.

I am under the impression that the President of Mexico is to be informed from Don Andres, or the correspondence he carries, that there is a danger of invasion from Americans (I am confident there is not) in this country, and to give some information relative to what they call driving Captain J. C. Fremont out of California; he is yet, I believe, surveying, or resting his horses in the interior.

When a translation of Capt. Fremont's letter was first given to the authorities, the words "and refuse quarter," were wrote I will give no quarter. The translator informed the Alcalde of the mistake. It may be so printed; in which case, you have a copy that should immediately follow in the Mexican papers, for which purpose, and that you may be well acquainted with all the circumstances, I send you copies of the Consular correspondence on the subject. About four hundred emigrants arrived in California in 1845. At the town of San José, eighty miles from Monterey, Don Andres Castillero had discovered a quicksilver mine; the ore produces from fifteen to sixty per cent. I have seen him, from an old gun-barrel, in thirty minutes, run out about twenty per cent. in pure quicksilver. This must be a great advantage to California.

I remain, sir, your most obedient servant.

To the Hon. Minister of Legation of the United States of America, City of Mexico.

That does not relate so much to this particular question. But the next does; it is directed to Major Gillespie, and is on page 2668 of the Transcript:

CONSULATE OF THE UNITED STATES OF AMERICA, } Monterey, April 23d, 1846.

SIR : Captain Montgomery of the " Portsmouth," being under sailing orders (the 1st or 2d instant) at Mazatlan, was waiting for the Mexican mail, when Commodore Sloat heard, per brig " Hannah," of the situation of Capt. Fremont, near San John's, and immediately dispatched the ship. She was twenty-one days from Mazatlan to Monterey.

Well now, we find the "Portsmouth," according to Mott, Talbot & Co.'s letter, at the port of Mazatlan on the first of April. Commodore Sloat was the flag-officer. He heard, as this letter of Mr. Larkin says, *per brig "Hannah,"* which arrived on the 1st of April, of the situation of Capt. Fremont. What does he do? He sends up the " Portsmouth " on the 1st of April; and she arrived here in some twenty-one or twenty-two days. That makes the dates correspond with the period when we say the voyage of the "Hannah " was performed, more or less, as near as could be expected.

Again, on the 2d of May, 1846, Mr. Larkin writes to Capt. Montgomery, of the "Portsmouth," as follows :

Five or six miles from the town of San José, and near the Mission of Santa Clara, there are mountains of quicksilver ore, discovered in 1845 by Don Andres Castillero, of Mexico, which I have twice seen produce twenty per cent. of pure quicksilver, by simply putting the pounded rock in an old gun-barrel, one end placed in the fire, the other end in a pot of water, for the vapor to fall into, which immediately becomes condensed. The metal was then strained through a silk handkerchief; the red ore produces far better than the yellow. There appears no end to the production of the metal from these mountains. Working of the quicksilver is but now commenced.

Now, are these letters genuine? I am addressing gentlemen whose intelligence no one can question. The books almost prove themselves. They are produced by the son of the Consul, taken from the archives of the Consulate ; having been kept by the Consul as the archives of his office. Reason and law alike invoke your Honors to give to these books, until they are contradicted, the credit of truth. But, it is supposed that it is barely possible to excite some doubt as to the authenticity of these several letters. Were the letters written, copies of which appear in these books?

Mr. Swasey swears—his testimony is given on page 2659 of the Transcript—that he was the clerk at the time these letters were written, and at the time when another letter, dated the 23d of April, 1846, was written; that he was called upon to testify in this case in behalf of the claimants by Messrs. Halleck, Peachy & Billings; that he was unwilling to testify until he should be able to refer to documents which would place the accuracy of his testimony beyond all doubt; that, as soon as an application was made to him to testify, he searched for the books of the Consulate, in which, according to his recollection, he was certain that letters would be found to answer all the inquiries that the counsel proposed to put to him.

Why, he was prudent, may it please your Honors. He found some of these letters, but he did not find all. He tells us that he found one of these two books. He got that from Mr. Larkin. But he was not satisfied still. Some four or five weeks, or more, after he obtained the book that my brother has before him—which book contained in part evidence confirmatory of his own recollections of the transactions to be inquired into—he heard incidentally that there was in brother Randolph's office another one of these books of the Consulate in which, according to his recollection, there was to be found other confirmatory evidence. He went to young Larkin, and they together went to brother Randolph's office and asked him about the book. Brother Randolph produced it.

Now, my brother Randolph seems to suppose that there was something in the conduct of Mr. Swasey—to use brother Randolph's own language—"excessively impertinent." It is not that what Mr. Swasey states, did not occur; for I asked my brother, as the Court will recollect: Do you mean to deny that what Mr. Swasey states in relation to the finding of the book, did not take place? No, says my brother. But for some cause or other—

Mr. Randolph—(interrupting). The word "finding" is used in relation to that which was never *lost*.

Mr. Johnson—It was "lost" to Mr. Swasey, and it was "lost" to the son of the Consul. I do not know what my brother Randolph may call "lost"; the book could not be *found*. I am of the opinion, that when a thing cannot be *found*, it is *lost*.

Mr. Randolph—The book was in my possession; the proper persons could come to me at any time to procure it.

Mr. Johnson—Of course, if they knew you had it.

Mr. Randolph—Mr. Larkin knew that I had it; he lent it to me.

Mr. Johnson—Mr. Larkin was dead. *He* could not go for the book. His son says that *he* did not know who had the book. His son so swears. I mean the son who came and testified in this Court. So far as *he* was concerned, as he swears, the book was lost.

Now, he goes to make the inquiry of Mr. Randolph, in whose possession he incidentally heard that this book was. This is not impeaching brother Randolph by any means. God forbid. My brother seems to think that everybody must have known where the book was. Oh, no! God forbid that everybody should know what is in my office—*all* the time.

I obtained the book, Mr. Randolph says, from the late Thos. O. Larkin, and Mr. Swasey obtains the book from Mr. Randolph's office. The question is asked by Mr. Peachy, with respect to these books:

Q. 10. Where did you obtain them?

A. I obtained the book entitled "Copies of Official Letters," from Mr. Frederick Larkin, and afterwards, with Mr. Frederick Larkin, called upon Mr. Edmund Randolph, at his office, and inquired for the book entitled "Correspondence with the Department of State." He pointed to a safe in the office, saying that he believed Mr. Henry Laurencel had locked up the book, and that Mr. Sellier had the key of it. I went to Mr. Sellier, who came, unlocked the safe, and Mr. Randolph delivered the book to Mr. Frederick Larkin, who then delivered it to me. This was after Mr. Thomas O. Larkin's death. Mr. Frederick Larkin was his eldest son, and one of his executors.

This is his answer to the question, and it is all true, as is conceded.

MR. RANDOLPH—Anybody else, with proper authority, could have procured the book.

MR. JOHNSON—You do not understand me. I admit that.

MR. RANDOLPH—I understand Swasey, very well.

MR. JOHNSON—If you understand him differently from what he said, you understand him differently from what I do. Whether *he* is given to *suspicion*, what *he* had in his heart, I do not know. I know the counsel (Mr. Randolph) needed that book for no purpose whatever. He had it; had a right to get it; and he kept it fairly; but he *had* it.

MR. RANDOLPH—But it is what his evidence is intended to convey—an impertinent reflection upon myself—that I allude to.

MR. JOHNSON—Well, I think not. At any rate, that does not show that he is not entitled to credit when he has got the book. If there is anything in this answer that intimates an idea that that book was kept away from the Court for any improper purpose, it is what I cannot see.

How came he to make the statement I have just read, may it please your Honors? Why, he had produced the books, or rather they were produced, and he was called upon to testify to their authenticity. After Mr. Peachy had got the books before him, and proved by his testimony, as far as possible, their authenticity, Mr. Peachy asked him, Where did you get them? He then gives the answer I have read.

MR. RANDOLPH—Why did he not stop there?

MR. JOHNSON—Because he *did* get them—one of them from Mr. Randolph. Suppose he said he got them from me; it would not be true. He said he got them from Mr. Randolph's possession, because they were in a safe in his office—properly there. The counsel cannot imagine I impute any impropriety to him.

Mr. Randolph—No. I speak only of the witness.

Mr. Johnson—I am speaking of the witness too. I never saw him until I came here; and I have no right to speak of him, except so far as the record speaks of his character. My friend, Mr. Randolph, comes to cross-examine him; and then he asks him, (page 2664):

Q. 26. You have said that you obtained one of these books (viz: "Correspondence with the Department of State,") from me, at my office. How many of the seven letters you have produced were copied from that book, and which of them?
A. Two. One is dated "Monterey, California, May 4th, 1846, addressed to the Hon. James Buchanan, Secretary of State, City of Washington." The other is addressed to the same person, dated "Monterey, March 5, 1848."
Q. 27. These two letters ought to be found in the State Department at Washington, ought they not?
A. They ought.
Q. 28. Have you never seen them printed, officially, among Senate or Executive documents, or both?
A. I don't recollect of having seen them.
Q. 29. Now, what was the object of your particularity in detailing the circumstances and manner of your obtaining that book, containing the correspondence of Mr. Larkin with the State Department, from me in my office, as in answer to question 10th?
A. Simply to answer the question by the counsel for the claimant.

Question 10 is in the direct examination; what I have just read.

His reply to that cross-interrogatory is:—"Simply to answer the question by the counsel for the claimant."

It makes no difference where it came from. It came from somebody. What does it prove? It proves the authenticity of all we rely upon.

Mr. Randolph—Certain letters are enumerated in that

question (26). Two of the letters are found in the book of which you are speaking. There are certified copies from the State Department, already in the record, of those two letters. They are also in the public document of the Senate of the United States, now before Mr. Benjamin; and those are the only two letters that upon examination your witness finds in the book.

MR. JOHNSON—He examined only a copy from the book.

MR. RANDOLPH—My question is: Which did you get from the book? supposing he copies or produces all that is in the book. That is the impression conveyed to my mind by the answer. What I object to now is, that upon his authority and no other, when the question has been put to him directly about that book, and he produces but two letters from it; the book shall now be produced to show others.

MR. JOHNSON—My brother says the letter of the 23d of April has been put there afterwards.

MR. RANDOLPH—I further say that production of those letters after that evidence, is in confirmation of what I said in the beginning, that it was a piece of impertinence on the part of the witness to go into particulars.

MR. JOHNSON—I do not suppose the witness had anything to do with our letter, improperly put in as you say, and whether put there improperly or not, there it is.

This book contains the official correspondence of the Consulate. This letter (of the 23d of April) is preceded by some business in relation to the Consulate, and is succeeded by letters to other persons, relating to the business of the Consulate, all in their order of succession and dates. That could not be unless the whole book was rewritten, and a forged transcription made of all the letters to be found in the original books; but it is admitted to be original, and is so introduced. The counsel is greatly mistaken if he supposes we rely on that book for anything improper. We have a right to rely on that book

when the witness speaks of the letter of the 23d of April, which
he finds amongst other letters produced, the authenticity of
which is not disputed because produced by the young man,
executor of his father; and if we find the same letter in the official correspondence between the Consul and the Department at
Washington, the authenticity of the correspondence is beyond
all doubt, because a great portion of the correspondence is to
be found in the archives at Washington.

Now, nobody says Swasey is not entitled to be believed.
What did Mr. Justice Hoffman say, in commenting on the testimony of Birnie in the injunction suit? Why, your Honor
said you *must* credit it, and said it on the clearest principles of
law, there being nothing on the face of his testimony so far in-
credible as to furnish positive evidence of its falsity. Your
Honor said, and I state it again, although wholly unnecessary :
" He stands impeached by any witness called up to disprove
the truth of the facts he states, or to prove that his general
character is such that credit cannot be given to his testimony."
That is Swasey's case. If he is not entitled to credit in Courts in
California, let those who know it come forward and testify. But
nobody has come. Standing uncontradicted and unimpeached,
he would be entitled, even if not confirmed, to absolute credit ;
and when not impeached or contradicted, and there is nothing
in his conduct to awaken doubts as to the accuracy of his testimony, your Honors are bound—for you have the means to
do it—to protect the witness, for it is the duty of the Court to
protect witnesses as well as counsel. Your Honors are bound
to look at such evidence before you as shows, that in any particular instance in which he is impeached there is no ground
for the impeachment. That evidence is to be found in what I
have just stated: that those letters of which he is testifying,
were to be found in *all* the books of the Consul.

MR. RANDOLPH—What I wish to say, is this : That under
the same circumstances, when a witness put on the stand, with
two books before him, produces letters out of the one book, not
in the other, if I had been on the other side I should have
adopted the course of the counsel who opened the case, referred

and relied only on the book which the witness produced, when referring to those letters.

Mr. Johnson—May it please your Honors, I am replying to the counsel for the Government, who has, on the authority of these letters, attacked the credit of the witness. If it is his duty to impeach him, it is my duty to defend him. I desire to see justice done. And I invoke the Court, when a witness is, without sufficient ground, impeached or attacked, to stand up and say that, so far as your Honors know, he is entitled to credit, and to hold a position among his fellow-men without reproach. I have done with him.

Well now, may it please your Honors, if all these facts are such that the Court cannot doubt, the only question that remains is: Do they constitute a title in the sense of the Act of 1851? Now, my brother Randolph has told your Honors that, with reference to the construction of that Act of 1851, we are confounding things entirely independent of each other. Title, he says, is one thing, the subject to which the title refers is another thing. We concede it. Land is one thing, the document by which you are to make out our right to stand upon the land, is another thing. He told us: "A camel carries burden, so does a horse; and a camel is not a horse, nor a horse a camel. A camel carries burden, and so does an ass; but a camel is not an ass, nor an ass a camel."

We might have carried the illustration further. An ass brays and makes a monstrous sensation, signifying nothing. A man talks and makes a monstrous noise, signifying nothing. Yet a man is not an ass, nor an ass a man.

Mr. Randolph—Very frequently he is.

Mr. Johnson—*You* may say that. *I* have no experience that way. I had not the slightest idea of applying it to you; or the slightest idea of applying it to myself. I am not so sure but I had somebody else in my eye [tapping Mr. Billings on the shoulder].

Now the question, under that Act of 1841, is—what is it

that your Honors are to deal with? What are you to confirm?
You are not to deal with lands in the abstract; you are not to
confirm the *lands*. Nature has done that. You are to deal
with a *claim* to lands. What does that involve? The *title* to
the lands. You are consequently to confirm the *claim*—to confirm the *title*. Whether the claim be of one interest or another
interest, is perfectly immaterial. The only question is, has the
particular claimant, as against the sovereignty of the United
States, a right to the possession of the land, at the time when
you are called upon to give him that right as against the United States? *That* is all. The extent of the right—whether it
is to last one year, or two years, or a thousand years, or for-
ever, to descend to his heirs in succession as long as he shall
have heirs, and then to revert to the Government of which he
may be a member, after his whole lineage shall be exhausted—
is perfectly immaterial. Has he a right *now?* and the Court
is called upon *now* to decide whether he has, or has not such
right. Has he a right to stand upon what is asserted to be
public domain? What does that depend upon? Has he, as
against the public, a claim authenticated by title which the
Court is bound, the public is also bound, to respect; a right,
as against the public, to hold the lands?

My brother considers this Act of 1851, as if it were confined
entirely to *fee simple claims;* or, to speak more correctly, to
claims for *fee simple interests* in lands. Why, to give such an
intention to the act, you will have to interpolate into the act,
those words. The extent of the interest is not defined or described by the act. The language of the act in connection with
the treaty of the 8th of February, 1848, is: Any claim derived
by *any* title from the Government from whom the United States
obtained the cession of the lands. Well, then, may it please
your Honors, if there existed in behalf of this claimant a right,
as against Mexico, to stand upon this mine to the extent of its
pertenencias, and to the extent of 3,000 varas, or to the extent
of two leagues, by *any* title derived from the Government of
Mexico, which that Government in conscience must have recognized and respected; so much of what was public domain,
to the extent of the interest so conveyed by the antecedent

owner to the individual proprietor, ceased to be public domain was not public domain, at the time of the treaty; not being public domain could not, by force of treaty, have been conveyed by the Government of Mexico to the United States; since it was impossible for that Government to convey that which it had not.

Well now, my brother supposes—and his whole argument is fallacious unlesss that supposition is true in point of law—two things. One of them is a fair subject for investigation I admit. In the other, he takes the ground taken by Mr. Commissioner Thompson in his dissenting opinion: That under the law of Mexico, at the time when this right was acquired, and at the moment when the Treaty of Guadalupe Hidalgo was negociated and ratified, the mining titles—for this is but one of all the mining titles—were simply licenses, which it was in the power of the Government of Mexico at any time to abrogate; which, as against the Government of Mexico, constituted no claim at all; which, as against the Government of Mexico, made the holder of the mine but a tenant at will, just as those citizens of California who are now digging over its mountains, and obtaining in its valleys the gold, are said to be tenants at will of the United States, having no legal right. But to that extent, my brother has not gone. Mr. Commissioner Thompson says, that there is something in the nature of our institutions which rendered the conveying of interests in these mining titles, impossible. (I do not use his words.) He considers the interest which the actual possessors of the mine have, as against Mexico, under these titles, as a mere political institution, an assertion of the sovereignty, suited to the form of government which Mexicans were living under at that time; but which failed after the cession, because unsuited to the form of government under which we were living at the time of the cession.

Now, as to both of those suppositions, a word or two. Mining titles in Mexico, such as Mexico could take away at any moment! Mere interest, depending upon the will of the grantor; good only as long as that will continued unchanged! Conveying no interest to the tenant; no possession binding the

conscience of the grantor not to dispute it! Governed by no
law obligatory upon the grantor, without the pale of legal
remedy!

Why, we say that by the ordinances under which Mexicans
lived, these mining titles were carefully issued and these mining
rights most religiously respected.

We say that commentators after commentators have exhausted their learning in commenting upon these several ordinances, for the purpose of showing what the right of the citizen
was; how it was to be acquired, how it was to be determined.
We say, that they tell us that is inheritable; liable to be sold
for the payment of debts; alienable; devisable. Who ever
heard of an estate at will descending to the heir-at-law? Who
ever heard of a tenant at will having the authority to dispose
of the estate, by deed? Who ever made sale of an estate-at-
will, or sold it for the purpose of discharging debts of the
tenant? Who ever heard, that at the death of the tenant,
that of itself did not determine the will?

The Supreme Court of the United States take a very different view of the effect of these ordinances. I read as part of the
decision—to be found, I think, in the brief of my friend on the
other side—in the case of Chouteau vs. Molony, reported in 16
Howard, pages 229–231:

Spain, at all times, or from a very early date, acknowledged
the Indians' right of occupancy in these lands, but at no time
were they permitted to sell them without the consent of the
King. That was given either directly under the King's sign-
manual, or by confirmation of the Governors representing him.
As to the mines, whether they were on public or private lands,
and whether they were of the precious or baser ores, they
formed a part of what was termed the Royal Patrimony. They
were regulated and worked by ordinances from the King.

Again:

By the law of the Partida (Law 5, Title 15, Partida 2, Rockwell, 126), the property of the mines was so vested in the King
that they were held not to pass in a grant of the land, although
not excepted out of the grant; and though included in it, the
grant was valid as to them only during the life of the King who
made it, and required confirmation by his successors.

* * * By a second ordinance of Phillip, all persons, na‧ tives and foreigners, were permitted to search for mines. It was declared that the finders of them should have a right of possession and property to them, with a right to dispose of them as of any thing of their own, provided they complied with the rules of the ordinance, and paid to the crown the seignor‧ age required.

And again :

He (the King) grants them to his subjects in *property* and possession, in such manner that they may sell, exchange, pass by will, either in the way of inheritance or legacy, or in any other manner to dispose of all their *property* in them, upon the terms they themselves possess them, to persons legally capable of acquiring. * * * The right of Indians to work the mines, upon their own account, was at one time questioned. It was determined that they could do so. (Law 14, Title 19, book 4, Collection of the Indies, Rock. 137.) And the mines discovered by Indians were declared to be, in respect to bound‧ aries, on the same footing, without any distinction, as those worked or discovered by Spaniards. Besides the other privi‧ leges secured by this ordinance to the owners of mines upon the public lands, they had the right to use the woods on moun‧ tains in the neighborhood of them, to get timber for their ma‧ chines, and wood and charcoal for the reduction of the ores (Rockwell, 82, sec. 12, ch. 13). Besides the privileges just stated, they were exempted from a strict compliance with the ordinance in respect to the registry of their mines. Indeed, every indulgence was given to them. Much care was taken to preserve for them their *property* in mines, and to give them the means of working them.

The King not only conveys to them a *property* in the mines, but, in the execution of a policy recommended to Spain by the colonies throughout all time, he is anxious that they should be encouraged in the discovery, and facilitated in the working of the mines. They could have the money or the means with which to manage and improve their property in the mines.

And now, may it please the Court, before you take the recess, let us see how the United States themselves, view it. And this you are bound to take notice of.

Property in mines is not under the protection of the treaty ! Property in mines is not intended to be observed and protected by the force of the Act of March 3d, 1851! Is *that* the view taken by the United States? They have got Arizona. How did they get it? By cession. What rights have they in the mines now in Arizona? Have they, as against anybody who has obtained title, whatever that might be, under the laws of Mexico, preceding the cession, the right to take the mines out of the hands of such individuals? Why, see what the Government are now doing with respect to New Mexico. I refer you to the recent instructions of the Commissioner of the General Land Office. Not having before me an official copy, I will read an abstract from a morning paper (the " Alta California.")

The Commissioner of the General Land Office, (Hon. Joseph S. Wilson), has dispatched important instructions to the United States Surveyor-General at Santa Fé, New Mexico, respecting mines. Parties had presented to the Surveyor-General papers claiming mining rights in virtue of " denouncement." The Commissioner refers to the mining system of old Spain, as transferring to Mexico after her separation from the parent country, in which rights were admitted by the Mexican Republic to work the mines upon discovery or denouncement. He shows that that system was not recognized by the laws of the United States, and orders the Surveyor-General to observe the policy which obtains in California, as not extending subdivisional lines of survey over either the mineral lands, or lands unfit for cultivation. He instructs the Surveyor-General that his duty in regard to claims is restricted to the reception of such only as are lawfully received from Spain and Mexico prior to the acquisition of the country by the United States, and the reception of donation claims under the laws of the United States.

And if prior, respect them! Why? The United States by virtue of the treaty or by conquest, got no right to interfere with them. The principle of universal justice, recognized now by the law of nations, prohibit it. Those laws of Mexico with reference to mines, made the mines private property. And the honor of the nation, the good name of the nation, is now pledged in the face of Christendom to secure to those who had claims to mines, fairly existing by virtue of Mexican law, antecedent to the cession of this territory—then Mexican—to the United States. Such titles cannot be acquired *now*, I admit. They are inconsistent with the policy of the United States. With reference, therefore, to mines undiscovered, or to mines abandoned and now a part of the public domain, or which have since become a part of the public domain of the United States, no individual proprietor can, by authority of Mexican law, or by observing the usages of Mexico, acquire title.

But if in any particular case, by means of these laws, ordinances, or usages, there were, on the 8th of February, 1848, a title in any Mexican citizen, or anybody else, to work mines within the limits of the territories ceded by force of the treaty to the United States—the hands of the United States are bound as an honest nation, in the face of the world, to leave them unharmed, to confirm them.

They have passed an act—3d of March, 1851—with that view. They have constituted a tribunal, supposed to be competent to decide justly on all such instances. More than that, they have given appeal to the District Court, in which they have all confidence. Supposing it barely possible that the District Court might not satisfactorily decide in all cases, they have given an appeal to the Supreme Court of the United States; and when they get there the Supreme Court say that such a controversy is not to be conducted in any *contentious* spirit, but on large, elevated views of national morality ; that all such contracts as were fairly binding on the conscience of Mexico are to be equally obligatory on the conscience of our own Government. Thank God! they have a conscience.

In the language of the Supreme Court in another case: " What will bind the conscience of a King, therefore, will surely bind the conscience of nations." The conscience of the King was bound when Mexico was a kingdom. The conscience of the dictator was bound, when Paredes was dictator. The conscience of Mexico, as a Republic, was bound, when, on the 8th of February, 1848, she ceded the territory which included this mine, to the United States. Good faith and good name, honor and justice, alike demand that the United States should be glad, aye, take an honest pride, through their judiciary, in securing by every means which they could procure for the purpose of accomplishing the object, all such titles antecedent, and making them, against the United States, as effective and good to every extent as they would have been good against Mexico.

MR. RANDOLPH—I simply wish to observe to Mr. Johnson, to save the trouble of replying to that point, that I am not particularly aware at this moment of the positions Mr. Commissioner Thompson has taken on this argument that mines duly acquired were not *property*, nor their possessors but tenants at will. My views on that subject are those of Chief Justice Taney, who says: "And whether there be any mines on this land, and if there be any, what are the rights of the sovereignty in them? are questions which must be decided in another form of proceeding, and are not subjected to the jurisdiction of the Commissioners or the Court, by the Act of 1851." That was my position.

MR. JOHNSON—I understand that. I will refer to it hereafter.

[The Court took a recess.]

—

MR. JOHNSON—It is objected, may it please the Court, that the construction for which we insist, of the Act of March 3d, 1851, is erroneous, because of the provision in the same act for the issuing of a patent to a claimant whose claim might be confirmed. And my brother upon the other side seems to suppose that there is in that provision a clear indication of the purpose of Congress to exclude from the operation of that act a title of this description. Now, I have two answers to make to that: *First*, that all that that section in the act provides, is that upon the claims being confirmed, a patent shall issue. He assumes that it is to issue in the ordinary form, because there is no provision under the laws of the United States, passed antecedently to the Act of 1851, for the issuing of any other kind of patent; and as the patent in an ordinary form, conveys, it is claimed, the *fee simple* in the land, it never could have been intended by this act—which provides for a patent—that a mining title should be confirmed, because a patent of that description would give more than is necessary for the security of a mining title.

Now, it must be very clear that the treaty covers a title of the miner in his discovery. If we are right as to this *property title* claimed to mines, you are to construe the Act of 1851, so as to make it embrace this case as well as every other case involving claims to real estate. And when the sections of the act which precede the particular section upon which my brother relies, construed by themselves, would cover a mining title, as well as any other title, when you come to consider the meaning of the subsequent section in relation to a patent, which upon its face does not provide that it is to give a *fee simple*, but merely directs that *a patent* shall issue to the claimant, you are then to say *that* secures only such a title in lands as has been confirmed to the claimant, whether it be *allodial*, *fee simple* or *conditional*.

The *other* answer to that, is this: The Court have nothing to do with the execution of that provision stated, which relates to the issuing of a patent; nothing whatever. Your duty is devolved upon you by force of the eighth section. That duty is, that upon any claimant presenting to you a title, derived from Mexico, to any interest—as we construe, to any land embraced within the treaty of cession,—you are to confirm it. If the Legislature of the nation, in that particular act, have not provided a means by which some other documentary voucher of that title is to be issued, as a patent for example, they will provide for it hereafter ; and the claimant will stand upon the title which he will have by force of your confirmation, your decree. Nothing can be plainer than that. And if we are right in the construction we give when we claim that the act before you covers this description of pro· perty, then it is perfectly evident that, if Congress have not provided a mode by which that title, when confirmed, is to be evidenced by some documentary evidence in Washington, it will be the duty of Congress hereafter to provide such a voucher.

We say, in behalf of the claimant, that, whether such a voucher can be issued now or not, under that law, to give us such evidence of that title, we are satisfied to stand upon your Honors' confirmation of the title under the very words of the act giving you that authority to act upon and to confirm the title if you think it a legitimate one.

My brother upon the other side, now and before, and the dissenting Commissioner, seem to suppose that there was to be found in the decision of Chief Justice Taney, in the case of Fremont, a clear indication that in the judgment of that Court, mines are not involved. That, I submit to the Court, with sincere respect for the judgment of the counsel as well as the dissenting Commissioner, is an entire misapprehension of that part of the opinion of the Chief Justice. The case before the Court was one involving simply the right to the land; that is all. A grant had been made to Alvarado, and of that grant Colonel Fremont had become the assignee. His claim was rejected by the District Judge, for reasons of very great weight. They were reasons supposed to be entirely destructive of the title, fatal to the title, in the judgment of the several Judges of the Supreme Court of the United States. The Chief Justice took a different view. Amongst other objections, an objection urged by the District Judge, in his opinion below, to the confirmation of that title, and taken by Mr. Attorney General Cushing in the Supreme Court—was this: That in Mexico there existed at the time of the cession to the United States, a right to the mines within the land granted to Alvarado; and consequently that if a patent issued—as it was to issue, in the event of Alvarado's title being confirmed to Colonel Fremont as the assignee of that title—as there was no distinction in the United States between the land itself, strictly speaking, and the mine, Colonel Fremont as the assignee of Alvarado, would obtain more than Alvarado could have obtained, or Colonel Fremont could have obtained as that assignee, under Alvarado's grant from Mexico.

The grantee of the land holds an interest in the land simply as such, for agricultural purposes. If there is found in this land included in the grant, minerals, those minerals belong to the Government; not by force of any contract between the grantee and the Government, but upon the ground that they are not under the laws of Mexico, transferred to the grantee. They remain still in Mexico, notwithstanding her grant of the surface. Well then, as Alvarado, if he had asked Mexico to confirm that grant, there having been no cession of the territory to the United States, would not have obtained the mines, it was impossible to confirm the grant by the United States; since the effect of that confirmation followed up by a patent of the United States, would be—there being no distinction as was alleged, between lands and mines in the laws of the United States—to transfer to Fremont as the assignee of Alvarado, a right to the mines, which were not transferred at all by Mexico by *her* grant of the lands.

And there was, apparently, force in it. See what is done, may it please your Honors. The question is yet to be tried. Fremont is now in possession *on* the mines, under that confirmation. He has got his patent. But Mexico did not give him the mines. *That* is very certain. The grant from Mexico did not give him the mines. How does he get them? He gets them, if he is entitled to them at all, by force of his patent from the United States; and as that patent is issued simply to confirm what Mexico gave, it will be a question *hereafter*, whether those mines do not still belong to the United States by force of the cession of the territory from Mexico to the United States, at a time when Mexico, as between herself and Alvarado or all claiming under Alvarado, was the proprietor of the mines. That question will come up, I suppose, to be decided. I have a very distinct impression as to what the decision will be, but it is unnecessary to mention it now.

Mr. Chief Justice Taney, speaking for the majority of the Court who coincide in this opinion, says (p. 165, 17 Howard):

In relation to that part of the argument which disputes Fremont's rights, upon the ground that his grant embraces mines of gold and silver, it is sufficient to say that, under the mining laws of Spain, the discovery of a mine of gold or silver did not destroy the title of the individual to the land granted. *The only question before the Court is the validity of the title*, and whether there be any mines on this land, and if there be any, *what are the rights of the sovereignty in them,* are questions which must be decided in another form of proceeding, and are not subjected to the jurisdiction of the Commissioners, or the Court, by the Act of 1851.

That is to say, that when a claimant presents himself before the Commissioners and afterwards before this Court, asking to have confirmed to him a title granting lands simply, you cannot try the question, whether there exists in anybody else by title derived from Mexico—whether that somebody else be the United States, or an individual proprietor—a right to the mines as contradistinguished from the land. *That* is to be decided *hereafter.* It is no issue involved in this case, as between the United States and the claimant to title under the grant to lands; because, whether there be mines or be not mines discovered, at the time of the grant or subsequent to the grant, is perfectly immaterial. The question submitted to the Court in such a case is, Is the grant of lands valid; and upon that question, I read again the language of Chief Justice Taney, in deciding it:

It is sufficient to say that under the mining laws of Spain a discovery of a mine of gold or silver did not destroy the *title* of the individual to *the land granted.*

That is *all* that they did, may it please your Honors. They went on to confirm the grant of Alvarado. Why they made it, what were the objections to the validity of that grant in other respects, how far they bear on the case—I shall have occasion by-and-by to examine; and I refer to it now to establish what I think is true, that my brother on the other side has misapprehended the opinion of Chief Justice Taney in that case. If there had been title derived from Mexico by Castillero or anybody else under the mining laws of Mexico, then that title must have been respected, because the Supreme Court say in the passage from which I have read you (16th Howard): "By the ordinances of 1783, in force, such a title as that was *property,* alienable, devisable, inheritable, and responsible for debts."

Why, this grant of the Mariposa region, including the immense mineral wealth which has since been discovered, which startles or rather surprises everybody, was not known at the time when Colonel Fremont bought, not even known to himself. The enterprise which he has exhibited in common with almost all the inhabitants of California, has brought Nature's · secret to light. Whether he is to have the benefit of that discovery which he is now practically enjoying (and which I trust he may ever enjoy), will depend upon what are the laws as between the grantee of the lands secured in his title by force of a patent issued under the Act of 1851, and anybody who shall attempt to get a title to the mines by any other proceedings. The question, as your Honors may have seen, if you attended to it in this bearing, has been met by anticipation of the authorities at Washington. The Commissioner of the Land Office acted, of course, upon the authority of the Executive Government in the instructions which I read to you just now. It is stated that, however true it is that the mining laws of Mexico, in respect to mining titles, are to be respected when there is a title derived under those laws anterior to the cession, yet such laws as are inconsistent with the existing policy of the United States as evinced by present legislation, are not to be regarded. You are, therefore, not to regard any denouncement or attempted denouncement, any registry or attempted registry to procure a title to the mines, as against the United States or anybody else in contradistinction to the title to the lands.

We give but one title under the laws of the United States. We grant but one title in the absence of particular legislation directing a different kind of grant. The title we give and the title we grant, without such special legislation, is a title to the land and everything in it, be it minerals, or be it clay, or sand, or anything else which constitutes the land.

So that I think it very clear, may it please your Honors, that there is nothing in that opinion, that part of the opinion— if there be anything anywhere else in the opinion—which bears on this part of the argument, which assists to the conclusion which my brother on the other side of this case desires you to come.

A word or two made in relation to the validity of the title, or rather in relation to the character of the estate obtained by the title, and I shall have done with this branch of the argument.

Why, so far from its not being considered as property, it was the preferred property in the estimation of Mexico. She lived by it. It was one of Nature's staples. It took the place of *American cotton, tobacco and grain.* To us the earth yields its fruit which enters into the immediate wants of man for sustenance. It is the instrument, the means of wealth, because it produces money where there is a surplus. But with *Mexico,* her mines were valuable as being, so to speak, the granaries of gold and silver ; and the value of these gold and silver minerals was important in the estimation of her interest and her glory. To promote both, and to beneficially develop the gold and the silver, she cherished the discovery and the working of quicksilver mines. Is it possible, may it please your Honors, that when that was her policy, when her policy depended upon individual enterprise which she had no means of advantageously carrying on herself, that she would be close or parsimonious in holding out inducements for such discoveries ? These secrets of Nature were hid in her mountain ranges, stretching from one end of her territory to the other. Her valleys, her rivers were supposed to be the receptacles of this treasure. How are they to be discovered? By individual enterprise. How is that individual enterprise to be obtained ? How is it to be promoted ? By holding out to the individal engaged in the work the prospect of gain. How is that done, according to her laws ? "Make the discovery and we pledge the honor of the nation that, that being done, if you will observe certain directions, in order to guard Mexico from any injury in any of her rights, or defeat in any of her hopes for which she desires the discovery to be made, you shall have *for all time,* undisturbed as against us, *property* in the mine, which you can give to your children, appropriate to the payment of your debts, or give to anybody whom you choose."

Well then, *prima facie,* we force an acknowledgment of our claims, without the production of any particular authority, without going to these ordinances which my brethren on the other side have referred to with so much ability,—which my brother Benjamin, with the aid of his clear digest, has condensed in such a manner that your Honors, I am sure, will agree with me in saying that the whole law on the subject of mining, as far as the questions in this case render it necessary to look at it, are so perspicuously presented that it is impossible to doubt that the presentation is right. If you doubted that, you have references to the admitted authorities upon such matters, by which you can easily and fully test the accuracy of the condensed statement. I say that it is unnecessary to go there.

The well known historical policy of Mexico, to be found in these archives, to be found in general history, which almost everybody sees, which everybody certainly hears—if he has heard anything or listened to anything concerning the well known policy of Mexico, concerning her mineral wealth—leads irresistibly to the conclusion that those who assist her in her mineral developments, could obtain under her laws a right to hold such mineral wealth to her exclusion, so far as her laws provide in the premises. So holding, it is in the discoverer's hands, PROPERTY.

Now, if the argument on the other side is sound, it would practically lead to this result. This whole title was consummated before the possession of the United States, and of course, before the conquest. It had gone through all the forms of Mexican jurisprudence. The whole Government of Mexico, and every man and woman in it, so to speak, recognized the validity of the title. The ownership was declared. Now $900,000 have been expended in developing it. It has carried joy through the whole of Mexico. But the development has cost this enormous expenditure. It has not yielded a dollar. I am now assuming a case; it has not yielded a dollar. It is about to yield. The holders of the title to it, which Mexico not only never dreamed of questioning, but which she could not question without violating her own honor, were just about to enjoy the benefits of their discovery, of their disbursements to make the discovery practically lucrative, and beneficial individually as well as politically. Mexico then is forced by the

United States—(because, in the language of Mr. Attorney General, we made for her a most advantageous treaty—we only got California, that's all—she may thank her stars that we did not get all of her territory !)—Mexico is forced to come forward and repudiate her promise and her pledge. The United States comes forward and says : We know all about it, the archives at Washington communicated to us the fact that the mine was discovered. The value of the mine was known, the expenditures were known. We know that as against Mexico you would have been permitted to hold on to the property and the revenues until you had recovered the amount of your disbursements, as long as it remained a source of profit and as long as it might lawfully descend, in the manner of other property, to your successors; but Mexico has ceded this property to us by a treaty which we say is advantageous to her; and now you must get off this property. We will have the benefit of your disbursements—we, the United States of America.

MR. PEACHY, (interrupting)—It was proposed in the Senate to devote the proceeds to the building of a Pacific Railroad.

MR. JOHNSON—It was *proposed ?*

MR. PEACHY—That was the proposition.

MR. JOHNSON—Well, I didn't know that anybody in the Senate had *proposed* anything like that ! A great many things are *proposed* in the Senate which do not strike everybody as the wisest plans in the world! A great many speeches are made in the Senate, that are *supposed* to have some few intellectual defects!

[Order was commanded in the court-room, many of the audience manifesting a disposition for loud laughter.]

MR. JOHNSON—(continuing) — "But let that pass!" Of course, I don't mean to be personal. Present company is always excepted.

It was *proposed*, you say, that the United States should take this mine, and with its revenues build a railroad from here to Texas! Why, what an honest operation that would be!

Castillero and those who claim under him, Barron, Forbes & Co. (Eustace Barron!) and others, were the holders of the mine, and we ought to thank our stars that they were. If Mexico had not been aided by their means the mine must have remained what the God of Nature formed it in the beginning—nothing but an unexplored vein. Nobody could tell whether valuable mineral was there or not, except the Indians who occasionally *rouge* their faces with it; in that respect anticipating civilization. (Present company always excepted)!

["Order" was again commanded in Court.]

Now, may it please the Court, could the United States, with any propriety, or, I was about to say, *decency*, in the case which I have supposed, insist upon taking a mine developed by means of the wealth of Mexican citizens, under a treaty in which they promised and pledged their honor to observe all species of private property derived from Mexico; knowing that by the laws of Mexico themselves, as between the private proprietor and Mexico, this property could not be appropriated to government use? Why, what does the treaty say? It says that "the holders of property under Mexico shall have the like guarantees." I may not use the exact words of the treaty, but very nearly—"the like guarantees enjoyed by citizens of the United States."

What are, amongst others, the guarantees furnished to citizens of the United States in reference to private property? It shall not be appropriated for public use *without full and adequate consideration* paid before the appropriation. It is a principle now of universal justice, recognized by every free government in the world, that private property cannot be taken in any other way, and cannot be taken at all except for a public purpose of a strictly legitimate character. The Government cannot take it from one individual and give it to another. The purpose for which it is to be taken is to be *public*. The indemnity to the full extent of the value of the property so taken, is to be paid by the public to whose purpose the property is about to be appropriated.

Is it possible, then, may it please your Honors, that when they agree to protect, by all the guarantees known to the Constitution of the United States, private property existing by title derived from Mexico, by any kind of title legally derived from Mexico, on or before the 2d of February, 1848—to throw around it all the guarantees that belong to individual property acquired here under the laws of the United States—that they can take it for any purpose, except a public purpose ; or that they can take it even then without first paying the entire value of it? And your Honors would be bound after such an attempt was made to issue an injunction to restrain the agents of the United States from touching the property.

Mr. Randolph—Do you apply that doctrine to Berreyesa's ranch ?

Mr. Johnson—I apply that rule of law to *any* property that is to be taken by the public for a public purpose. I do not know that the Attorney General intends confiscating Berreyesa's ranch, or anybody else's ranch. He lets them stand unquestioned.

All that I know, and all that I mean to say in this connection is, that this is "property" under the laws of Mexico, and inasmuch as Mexico recognized it as *property*, and that the territory comes into the United States incumbered with this interest as *property* which, according to the plighted faith of the United States, is to be protected by the United States, with all the guarantees thrown around any description of *property* by the institutions of the United States.

I leave the subject, may it please your Honors—that branch of the argument.

I referred yesterday, at about the close of the sitting of the Court, to a point of fact as to the grant of the two leagues ; and here is the original paper before the Court for inspection.

Your Honors will see in what in Spain they call the rubric to the signature—a private mark which, as I am given to understand, is common to all official signatures. Here it is, may it please your Honors—[holding up a paper]—here is the original. It has a stamp at the head of it, showing the character of the paper.

I have before me, of the date of the 24th of March, 1846, another document, professing to have been signed by Castillo Lanzas, of the authenticity of which there can be no doubt.

Now, your Honors will find, by comparing the paper of the one with the other, that the paper is identical; and, by looking at one or two other archives in evidence before you, you will find that the paper used at the time when this grant was made—as is proven not only by this grant, for the authenticity of this being disputed, we cannot rely upon *that* as any evidence to prove all the papers in the archives of about the same date—are identical. The paper used before this time, that is, the paper used in the previous year, and which was now exhausted, bears a different stamp.

[Mr. Johnson hands the papers to the Court.]

His Honor, Mr. Justice Hoffman, in giving his opinion in the Limantour case, very properly relied upon the difference between the paper to be found in the archives at the period when the grant to Limantour professed to have been made and the paper upon which those grants were written. His Honor came to the conclusion—to which he was almost forced to come—that that fact of itself proved that the titles produced by Limantour were fraudulent, as contradistinguished from the genuine.

Now, if the argument is a sound one—and no one can doubt that it is a sound one—it ought to operate both ways. If the difference between the paper in the Limantour case would lead you not only to doubt, but to come almost to the certain conclusion, that Limantour's grants were fraudulent, the identity of the paper in the Lanzas grant with the paper used in the admitted archives at the date of the Lanzas grant, should be equally conclusive evidence to show that the Lanzas grant is a fair and honest grant.

The Government cannot use evidence of that sort merely for

the purpose of accomplishing their own ends. If they invoke the archives, as they did in that case, for the purpose of proving that the particular grant in question was fraudulent, characterized in their hands as evidence of fraud, relying upon the difference of the paper when, in 'that case, the archives are produced to tell a different story, to indicate wrong in the claim for title, it shocks all reason and all justice; it does violence to all notions of right, to insist that we shall not, in this case, argue the truth of this title on a like basis—the precise similarity of the paper in the case before us.

But, may it please your Honors, there is other confirmatory evidence about which there can be, as I submit, no sort of doubt. We have archives here. There were local bureaus, local departments, acting under the authority of Mexico, here in California. The existence of these authorities became necessary in order to enable Mexico to carry out her policy here. Everything could not be done in the City of Mexico. Local power has to be given. Who is to be dealing with the property belonging to her in California? In California there might be discovered mines of inexhaustible wealth, of immense importance to her own prosperity. Her laws required that certain forms should be gone through with before individual titles could be secured in such mines, for her protection as well as for the protection of the grantee. She has two things in view: first, to encourage the discovery of mines; secondly, to protect her own interests therein. In order to do both, she must have in the locality where the property may be discovered, authorities to superintend the execution of her laws, so as effectually to promote the object of securing herself as well as of securing to the discoverer the benefit of his discovery. She had "ALCALDES." She had no other judicial officials here at the time.

We maintain, whether correctly or not, your Honor's will decide, that at that time—because there was no other local authority holding a judicial power competent to carry out the mining laws so as to secure to the discoverer his mining title—the *Alcalde* possessed that authority.

I assume now, in passing, that in that argument we are wrong. That makes no difference in the view in which I am now bringing the matter before the Court. Everybody supposed he had, or at least there was nobody who had that power, unless *he* had it. Now, we show that Castillero proceeded before that Alcalde with all these titles, so far as it was necessary to have in the archives here the evidence of their existence. Those are all proved by the production of the archives. Are they so proved?

Here we have, may it please the Court, the original papers, proved by witnesses, as I will show you in a few moments. Now, I assume this to be an original [holding up a paper.] There is between the fourth and third lines, at the close of the paper, an interlineation, running the whole width of the paper, coinciding in length with the lines of the paper. Who put it there? Who put it there? We say, Castillero. When? Whilst he was here. When was that? In 1846; on or before the 4th of April, 1846. Why? We say that it must have been before the 4th of April, 1846; because, on that day he went away and has never returned. The proof is, that this paper remained in the archives from the time it was there deposited until it was produced here.

Now, we say that this is Castillero's handwriting. Is it? My brother Randolph says, that with all the respect he entertains for the judgment of Mr. Hopkins, he must deny the assertion that this is Castillero's handwriting. Now, as far as my brother Randolph recollects, this handwriting is proved to be Castillero's only by the testimony of Mr. Hopkins, who says that he *believes* it to be the handwriting of the said Castillero. Mr. Hopkins thinks so: he believes it. Well, that proves nothing, except Mr. Hopkins' opinion. He never saw Castillero write. He judges from a comparison of signatures of the same description, and of writings which he understands to be the writings of Castillero. Comparing what he presumes to be the real writing of Castillero with this interlineation, he is brought to the *belief* that that interlineation is in the handwriting of Castillero.

But that is not all: my brother had forgotten that there was other evidence. Turn to page 3069 of the Transcript. Hopkins, in his certificate dated Sept. 27th, 1860, says:

7

And that I think the first page of said document is in the handwriting of Andres Castillero; and that the following interlined words, to wit—

I won't read the Spanish that follows, for fear of shocking the classical ears of *some* of my friends, who fancy that they are particularly classical, so far as the Spanish is concerned. Mr. Hopkins quotes the Spanish. And what follows in this certificate?

—Found on the second page of said document, between the sixth and seventh lines, counting from the bottom of the page, I think are also in the handwriting of said Andres Castillero.

Now, if you will turn to pages 3042, 3043, you will find this stipulation, to which Mr. Randolph affixed his signature. It is dated the 1st of October, 1860. It was filed on the 4th of October.

"It is further stipulated and agreed that M. G. Vallejo will prove the handwriting of, and the signature to Exhibit Castillero No. 5." This is a letter from Andres Castillero to Alexander Forbes, dated January 14th, 1847. But this is not all. I am now dealing with the interlineations on this document which is marked "Exhibit J. Y. No. 1, W. H. C.," and the question who wrote them. The stipulation goes on:—"And it is further stipulated that General M. G. Vallejo will prove the handwriting of Castillero in the parts of Exhibit J. Y. No. 1, W. H. C., which, in the written statement of R. C. Hopkins, he says he *believes to be in the handwriting of said Castillero.*"

Brother Randolph did not give any intimation at that time that he would not consider that to be true which was proven by General Vallejo.

MR. RANDOLPH—That is another matter.

MR. JOHNSON—We told you at the time what we intended to prove. You were weak enough to sign this stipulation and we take the advantage of it. Of course the United States can say that our witness is not to be believed. But here is the agreement. We might have called up and examined General Vallejo.

MR. RANDOLPH—I would not have cross-examined him.

MR. JOHNSON—I think that that is doubtful.

MR. RANDOLPH—I can refer you to a number of witnesses whom I did not cross-examine.

MR. JOHNSON—That is better. You are obliged then to come to the conclusion that the proof was so strong that you could not contradict it or explain it, or, by any sort of hocus-pocus, get clear of it.

MR. RANDOLPH—Or get over or under it?

MR. JOHNSON—Yes; and all that sort of thing! When I have a great many things to say and little time to say them in, I bundle them all up in—"and all that sort of thing." I don't think that it was altogether right to entrap my brother Randolph in this way; I don't wonder that he is disposed to make some complaint!

Now a word or two on another point.

These papers are all true. All that we say, is true. The mine was discovered. The mine was registered. It was registered for the purpose of securing the title. It has been sold; and the purchasers have bought and sold shares in it, upon the faith of that title. That which they have seen they believe. What have they seen? What do they know occurred before the 2d of February, 1848? It is discovered, denounced, registered, and efforts were made in Mexico to secure a title. Disbursements are made in Mexico on the faith of that title. What does the United States do? We are now in a Court of Equity, in which the principles of equity are to govern. What does the United States know?

Communications made by Mr. Larkin, an officer of the United States, to Washington, tell that Government that Castillero is in possession of this mine before the United States dreamed of acquiring California by conquest! I say, the proper representative of the United States *here*, in California, long before the treaty of the 2d of February, 1848, by which we acquired this country, in his official communications, on file in Washington, at the date of that treaty and long before, had informed our Government *that Castillero was working this mine as its owner, that he claimed to be its owner, that he had acquired a right, interest or title to it under the mining ordinances under the laws of Mexico, just as any one else acquired a right or title to a mine anywhere else in Mexican territory; and, moreover, that this mine was of almost incalculable value.*

Did Mexico interfere with his working, or deny his claim of ownership to this mine between the time of its discovery and the date of the treaty? Oh, no; that Government not only recognized and confirmed his claim of ownership, but also did everything in its power to encourage and facilitate his working this mine. And what does the United States now say with respect to such mining rights acquired prior to that treaty in New Mexico? Our Government says, through its Commissioner of the General Land Office: "I do not interfere with mining titles acquired prior to the acquisition of the country; *they* are beyond the power of the United States; I only interfere with those who attempt to get mines in the ceded territory under and by virtue of Mexican laws now no longer in force there, and contrary to the laws of the United States!"

But, it is said, although Castillero may have had *a* title in point of *fact*, he knew, or ought to have known, that he had no fully vested title in point of *law*, at the date of the treaty; and that although the United States *knew* at the date of the treaty that he had a claim or pretended title to this mine, they knew or believed that that title was not a complete *legal* title. Is that to defeat the claim?

Your Honor, Judge Hoffman, in commenting upon a decision of the Supreme Court, lays it down as a principle of law, too clear to be disputed, that where anything has occurred before the cession, before the conquest, constituting an equity as against the Mexican Republic, it creates, as against the United States, an inchoate title which is to be confirmed by his Court under the provisions of the Act of 1851, because he is directed to be governed by the principles of *equity!*

And now the United States, with the knowledge of our discovery of this mine, of our working it, of our claim of ownership under Mexican laws and usages, with the knowledge that Mexico permitted and encouraged all this—as is proved by their own archives at Washington, proved by the archives of the State Department, whose special function it is to negotiate treaties—the Attorney General, *now*, speaking in the name of the United States, with a knowledge of that fact, wishes to stand,—not upon the *treaty* but upon words in the *projet* of the treaty which were stricken out by the United States, or upon the words of the Mexican Commissioners who negotiated that *projet* of a treaty, saying that no grants had been made subsequent to the 3d of May !

It is to be supposed that the contents of these archives were known to the officers of our Government who were charged with negotiating and ratifying that treaty. And with this knowledge, what did they do with respect to this tenth section? *They struck it out*, thereby saying, that if any grants had been made subsequent to the 3d of May, such grants were to be put upon the same footing as if no such assertion had been made by these Mexican Commissioners. What faith did *they* put in the assertions of these Mexican Commissioners? Did *they* attempt to limit the honor and good faith of the United States towards private persons by any stipulations based on these assertions? And Mr. Marcy and Mr. Cass, have *they* attempted to bind Mexico by this rejected part of this *projet* of the treaty? Did *they* attempt to hold Mexico to an account for erroneous statements of her Commissioners—statements which *they*, from the evidence in their own offices, knew to have been erroneous? *They* were honest men, may it please the Court. Great men were they ; and what is still better, *honest men*—men alive to the *honor* of their country !

Again, suppose these Commissioners had stated what they knew was untrue ; should their false statements operate to defraud Castillero, and those claiming under him, of their rights in this mine? Why, there is not a Court of Equity which, as between individuals, would not at once declare that a party standing in relation to property of this description in which the United States stand, according to the evidence here offered by the United States, had no right to interfere with Castillero's title, which would not, by injunction, prohibit such a private party from attempting to interfere with such a title.

"Whatever," in the language of Mr. Justice Baldwin, in pronouncing a decision in another case in the Supreme Court: "whatever," in the language of Mr. Justice Hoffman, in pronouncing his decision in several of these land cases, "has occurred in the ceded territory prior to the cession, binding the conscience of the antecedent sovereignty, binds us."

God forbid, says Mr. Justice Baldwin, that the conscience of the Republic is not as pure as the conscience of a Monarchy!

I might, therefore, as far as the exigencies of this case are concerned, surrender to the objections to the legality of that title,—admit that the whole proceedings are illegal. Mexico had no right to rely upon that, may it please your Honors. We went upon it, believing that they were correct. Mexico told us by her own conduct that they were correct. The conduct of the Alcalde, giving us judicial possession, was affirmed in all its parts. She granted to us two leagues, congratulated her people that the mine had been discovered and was about to be developed by these very men, and represented it to the Congress of Mexico. It carried joy, as far as such a discovery could, to every public man in the State. She never has attempted to forfeit it.

And what says the Supreme Court of the United States, in the case I read your Honors yesterday for another purpose? (Case of Fossatt, 21 Howard):

The object of this inquiry was *not to discover forfeitures or to enforce rigorous conditions.* The declared purpose was to authenticate *titles*, and to afford a solid guarantee to *rights.*

If Mexico had a conscience, which prohibited her from enforcing forfeitures, it is not the purpose of the United States to do that which Mexico would have been ashamed to do!

And yet that is precisely what the United States are now attempting to do. What is my brother's objection, amongst other things, to the validity of this title? That it is not *vested.* It is not a case of forfeiture, he says; it is a failure to fulfill the conditions by which the title itself is to vest originally, conditions *precedent.* I illustrate it by applying his argument to part of what has been done. In order to secure a full development of the mine, you say that it really is to be worked, and that the public is to get the benefit of it. It is made the duty of the local officer, before he grants juridical possession, to see that the well, which the law prescribes, is of certain dimensions in width and depth. The width is prescribed, as is the depth. Now, the argument of my friend on the other side is, that that well must first exist before the title can vest.

MR. RANDOLPH—The ordinances say so.

MR. JOHNSON—I will admit that, for the sake of argument. But what else do they say ? They say they constitute as their representative an officer to pass upon that question. How deep is it to be ? So many feet,—say thirty feet, and about four and a half wide. Who is to pass upon that, as between Mexico and the claimant ? Castillero presents himself and says: I have a well thirty feet deep, and four and a half feet wide. He takes the Judge—the umpire to pass upon it, as between himself and the Government—and that umpire decides that that well complies with the ordinances ; that it *is* thirty feet deep and four and a half feet wide ; and he gives him juridical possession. Some busy, prying body who wants to get the mine thereafter, after we have gone into possession of the property on the faith that we have got the title, because it has been determined by the proper officer that we have complied with that part of the ordinances, goes up on that mountain, puts down *his* measuring rod, and finds that, instead of being thirty feet deep, it is twenty-nine feet eleven inches, and that it falls short one inch of the width required. What a chance there is for a fortune! There is a failure to dig out an additional inch! Well, who is to try that? Why, the man who relies upon the judgment of the Alcalde—Castillero, for example, in this case —will be very apt to believe that the Alcalde has measured that correctly. The question is brought before your Honors, or some other judiciary. I will imagine the present contestants to be the men. Justo Larios or Laurencel—(I don't want to say anything against *him;* I am afraid it might get to Montgomery street. What I say of *him,* I wish to be understood as said in a *whisper*)—tries to denounce the mine—to get the title to the mine; and there is a contest between him and Castillero as to whose is the mine. Castillero comes and says— Why, it is mine; I say it is thirty feet deep and four and a half feet wide. The Alcalde has said so; I acted on the faith of that—on the faith of the judgment of the Alcalde. But, your Honors say, that won't do. It must depend on the "*fact*." And then we want a survey, and your Honors are asked to go to the mountain and plunge down and see for yourselves if an inch is wanting; and just as you discover the omission of an inch, just so will you decide that the title is in Castillero or the man contesting it !

May it please your Honors, the very moment it is ascertained that the object of the provision transferring the authority to the Alcalde, is to transfer it to him as a *judicial* authority, his judgment is conclusive. It cannot be *collaterally* inquired into. How is it to be *directly* inquired into? If the question thereafter arises as between the denouncer or register and the Government, and the Government think it is material that the ordinances should be complied with in reference to the well to the letter, why, they will refuse to confirm what has been done.

But in this case they confirm, provided you believe their archives. They sanction the juridical possession. They make the grant; they approve the conduct of the Alcalde; and their attention was specifically called to it by Castillero him- self. He had been given three thousand varas. The authority of the Alcalde to make a grant to that extent did not exist. It was necessary therefore to get a sanction to what had been done from the Government itself. That was done, as we say, so that the action of the Alcalde, involving all the principles in which the legality of that action is called in question now, was brought before the Supreme Government, passed upon by the Supreme Government, and confirmed by the Supreme Government. What right has the United States, who have derived title from Mexico after that confirmation, to go behind that confirmation, and hold that *she* will not be bound—al- though she had no right to say anything upon it at the time— because she is satisfied that the judgment of the Alcalde upon the disputed point, and the judgment of the Supreme Government of Mexico, afterwards, were erroneous?

Now, may it please your Honors, I have wearied you much more than I could have wished, and I conclude this part of the argument, therefore, with saying that, looking to the evidence, as far as I have examined it, written or oral, the mine *was* discovered; the mine *was* denounced; the mine *was* registered; the title to the mine *was* granted by Mexico in all the forms of her laws, as applicable to the grant. Two leagues *were* also granted.

But there is, as it is supposed, in the record evidence to show that all these title papers are "forged, fraudulent, fabricated, false, and antedated; null and void, and of no effect whatever." I should like to know who prepared that bill. I should consider him a professional curiosity. I am sure it was not done here. A gentleman who puts so many interrogations would not be found repeating so much as that bill does!

Now, I have a word or two to say in relation to the fraud supposed to be established by these letters.

Who is the man that brings it forth to the light of day? Jas. Alexander Forbes. Who is he? Who would believe *him?* Not *I*, says my friend Mr. Randolph.

MR. RANDOLPH—Not his *own* statement.

MR. JOHNSON—Not his *own* statement! Much more likely to believe it was untrue because he said it! Well, he (Randolph) surrenders him to our mercy; and he has received it. I do not propose to extend it any further. *He* is not to be believed. So much I suppose I can say on the authority of the counsel for the United States. Nothing, therefore, is to be credited at all, as bearing upon the question which I am now to discuss, but *his* letters, and the letters produced by *him*, coming from Alex. Forbes, Barron, Forbes & Co., or William Forbes.

Now, what is the question? Are the title papers upon which we rely now, and upon which we originally relied, "false, forged, fabricated and antedated?" How many frauds were contemplated by James Alex. Forbes—how the proposition to perpetrate them was listened to by anybody connected with the mine—is perfectly immaterial to the question before your Honors, except so far as that fact bears on the integrity of the papers upon which we rely.

I might as well state the law before I proceed to the facts. I have not the original case before me, but it is to be found in 4th Peters, pp. 295–310. Mr. Justice Baldwin, giving the opinion of the Court in the case of United States vs. Arredondo (6 Peters, page 716), declares them to be incontrovertible, and repeats them at length:

First. That actual fraud is not to be presumed, but ought to be proved by the party who alleges it.

Second. If the motive and design of an act may be traced to an honest and legitimate source equally as to a corrupt one, the former ought to be preferred. This is but a corollary to the preceding principle.

Third. If the person against whom fraud is alleged should be proved to have been guilty of it in any number of instances, still if the particular act sought to be avoided be not shown to be tainted with fraud, it cannot be affected by these other frauds, unless in some way or other it be connected with or form a part of them.

Now, I refer your Honors to an opinion pronounced by the Supreme Court at the last term—to be found in 22 Howard, page 315—in the case of the United States vs. West, conducted by my brother who is before me, in behalf of the claimant. The Attorney General of the United States got it into his head that a title, fair and valid as against the United States by title derived from Mexico, became forfeited to the United States by reason of a fraudulent attempt afterwards to include within that title more land than the title itself embraced. The Supreme Court say the fraud was proved beyond all doubt; yet they tell us this:

We have only to observe that the *fraudulent* attempts to enlarge the grant *were made after California had been ceded* to the United States, and though the proof of it is undeniable and was an attempt to *defraud* the United States, that cannot *take away* from the wife and children of West their claim to the *grant which was made to him before California had been transferred by treaty.*

Now I proceed, may it please your Honors, to inquire if there is in the evidence of those letters anything to lead the judgment to believe that this title upon which we stand was forged.

Let us take up some of these letters.

The letters of Alexander Forbes produced by James Alex. Forbes—not willingly, for he was terribly distressed when they were produced against his will !—commence at page 382 of the Transcript. I have not time to read all. The first letter is dated May 11th, 1846, and speaks of the mine, saying :

If quicksilver mines of value are discovered, it would be of immense interest for Mexico, as, owing to the scarcity and high price of this article, the poorer silver mines of Mexico cannot be worked.

We will pass over the other letters till we come to those which are supposed to contain the evidence of fraud. James Alex. Forbes says—and your Honors will find it at page 391 —that he left at Tepic with Alexander Forbes, a memorandum of the documents which he thought ought to be obtained. He says he left that in May, 1849.

What are those documents ? (Page 391):

Memorandum of the documents which Don Andres Castillero will have to procure in Mexico :

First.—The full approbation and ratification by the Supreme Government of *all the acts* of the Alcalde of the District of San José, in Upper California, in the possession given by the said officer *of the Quicksilver mine* situated in his jurisdiction *to Don Andres Castillero in December*, 1845.

That admits the existence of the original paper. He thought that of itself would not be sufficient, that there ought to be obtained a false approbation and ratification of that paper by the Supreme Government. What else does he want ?—

Second.—An absolute and unconditional *title of two leagues of land* to Don Andres Castillero, specifying the following boundaries : on the north by the lands of the rancho of San Vincente and Los Capitancillos ; on the east, south and west by vacant lands or vacant highlands.

Third.—The dates of these documents will have to be arranged by Don Andres; the testimony of them taken in due form, and besides certified to by the American Minister to Mexico, and transmitted to California as soon as possible.

Now I pass by the inquiry, whether that memorandum was left there or not. I have no idea that it was; but I admit it was, for the sake of argument. How does that prove that those papers we rely on here were not genuine? He (J. A. Forbes) wanted others; why, you will see by-and-by. And he suggests what others he did want. The first was one emanating from the Government of Mexico *itself* fully proving and ratifying what the Alcalde had done in 1845. Well, *he* had done what the denouncement and registry proves he had done. He had given juridical possession; he had attempted to transfer to the discoverer of the mine 3000 varas. What else does he want?

There had been, as we say, a grant of two leagues before the date of this memorandum. What was that grant upon its face? To whom was it directed? What has been done by the party to whom it is directed? It was a grant of two leagues; directed to the Governor of California, who was to put the grantee in possession of the two leagues. And there was an impression, that, standing by itself without any action on the part of the Governor of California delivering possession of the two leagues, it conveyed no title. But there was a place where a title *could* be obtained; that place was Mexico. The Supreme Government, at the date of that grant, had the authority to convey. They purposed to convey. Their conveyance was such a form that it did not (as he thought) operate as a conveyance; and now the property having passed, or being about to pass into the possession of the United States, it cannot be carried out as the Government of Mexico designed. What, then, do I want, says James Alex. Forbes. What he wants admits an antecedent grant, as your Honors will see on criticizing the second clause of the memorandum:

An *absolute* and *unconditional* title of two leagues of land to Don Andres Castillero, specifying the following boundaries—

What "two leagues of land?" The two leagues of land

contained in the dispatch of Castillo Lanzas, made on the 23d of May, 1846. *That* was a grant in colonization, a *conditional* grant. *That* was not an "absolute grant." It looked to the occurrence of something to be done thereafter, in order to give title to the land granted to the grantee. "What you must have, must go back and be dated at the time that supposed conditional grant was made. You must get from that Government a grant upon its face of the two leagues now held under a form of grant. You must get a grant, which upon its face shall be absolute and unconditional." That is what he wanted. But that is not all. The criticism which I am about to make on the letter I am about to read, will be equally applicable to other letters with which I will not fatigue the Court.

We produced the letter of May 5th, 1847; which your Honors will find at page 842. Why we produced it I will tell you in a moment. It is a letter from James Alex. Forbes, and its authenticity is not doubted. He admitted it himself. What does he say in it?

I have done everything that I possibly could do for the advancement of your views in this undertaking, and have communicated to Mr. Walkinshaw all the information relative to the necessary measures that must be taken in order to preclude the possibility of suffering an intrusion by the Americans, or by any other persons who may find a pretext for litigation, and I now lay before you my views, that you may see the necessity for immediate action. It is of the most vital importance to obtain from the Supreme Government of Mexico, a positive, formal, and unconditional grant *of the two sitios of land conceded to D. Andres Castillero*—

When conceded? Before the date of this letter of the 5th of May, 1847. What concession had been made? What is the date of the concession? The concession made by Castillo Lanzas, dated 23d of May, 1846 :

—" of the two sitios of land conceded to D. Andres Castillero, *according to the decree appended to the contract* "—[which was then before him, and he had evidence of it]—"and also an unqualified ratification of *the juridical possession which* WAS *given of the mine by the local authorities of this jurisdiction*, including, if possible, the three thousand varas of land *given in that possession* as a gratification to the discoverers."

That is precisely what the juridical possession attempted to do.

The documents should be made out in the name of D. Andres Castillero and Socios. I think that it will not be difficult to obtain these documents, on making known to the Supreme Government that this Departmental Government is completely " acefalo," in consequence of which *the possession of the two sitios ordered to be given by the dispatch of Señor Castillo Lanzas* has not been obtained, and cannot be obtained, nor even mentioned without imminent risk of opposition on the part of the American Government in this Department. It is indispensable that the title and ratification of possession should be of *the date of the decree of Señor Lanzas.*

Now, stopping there, is it not palpable that he was finding fault, suggesting doubts as to this title, not upon the ground that the title which we now produce was not fairly obtained, but because, although fairly obtained, it had not positively passed title?

First. Because upon the face of the Lanzas grant the title was made to be dependent upon the subsequent delivery of possession, as a condition precedent to the vesting of title.

Second. Upon the ground that the grant of the Alcalde, by whom the juridical possession of 3000 varas was given as a gratification to the discoverer, was defective because of want of authority on the part of the Alcalde to make any such grant.

Go to Mexico! These papers are genuine. I admit that; nobody can doubt that. I have in the contract of ratification now before me, evidence of the Lanzas grant. I know it was dated on the 23d of May, 1846. I know the Alcalde had given juridical possession in December, 1845. I know all that. But such is the condition of the Government here, that won't do. The Government here is completely " acefalo;" and because it is so, possession is not to be obtained of the two leagues conceded by the Castillo Lanzas decree, cannot be obtained, and it will even be dangerous to mention that there exists, in fact, any such dispatch. Go, therefore, and if you can, get the Government to give you instead a " positive, formal and unconditional grant" of the two *sitios*. Also, if you can, get an unqualified ratification of the juridical possession which was given of the mine and the 3000 varas as a gratification to the discoverer.

Then he suggests what will be necessary to secure the titles. And he goes on further:

With respect to the ratification of the contract between yourself and Mr. Macnamara, for the *habilitacion* of the mine, as promised by Don Andres Castillero, I, as attorney or procurator of the two Robles, send that document, in which I ratify (in their name) the contract, and make allusion to the privileges conceded by the Mexican Government to the owners of quicksilver mines; for, in lieu of those privileges, it was *expressly stipulated* by Don Andres Castillero and his socios, that they should all participate *in the two sitios of land to be asked* of the Departmental Government.

Now come to the next letter; to be found at page 844. This is dated October 28th, 1849:

I have been detained here until the present moment, occupied in carrying out the arrangements explained to B., F. & Co., in my letters to them of yesterday's date, and to which I beg to refer you. My reasons for purchasing the land of that part of the farm of the Berreyesas which I pointed out (to Mr. Alexander Forbes and yourself) on the map of New Almaden, are: *First.* Because I fear the destruction of some important papers of *the original registry of the mine*, and which I believe will be effected, or, that on those very *documents of registry* a question will arise as to the legality of the possession; *Second.* Because no posterior grant of the Government could authorize the occupation of the land of the Berreyesas, on which the mine is declared to be situated in *the original espediente of registry*.

Then he admits *the original espediente of registry!*

Third, Because I am convinced that Walkinshaw and his party have endeavored to make the purchase of the land, fearing that the denunciation will prove fruitless, in all of which cases they will come forward as the owners of the land comprising the mine and hacienda. Therefore, it is of great risk for me to disregard the claims of the Berreyesas, and to set up a dispute upon boundaries, when I am uncertain as to the production of the documents held by Walkinshaw, and of the validity (in the accursed Courts of this country) of the original registry of the mine.

He meant *State* Courts, I suppose.

MR. RANDOLPH—He meant the "accursed Courts" of 1849.

MR. JOHNSON—It applies as much now, as then, I suppose! Now to page 846.

I now desire to call your attention to the following important matter. In order to secure the possession of *the land which was granted to Castillero and his associates upon the mining possession of New Almaden*, you must bear in mind that *that document* was not recorded in this country, but that it remains in the hands of Walkinshaw; that in all probability it will be destroyed, if it has not been destroyed already. That in view of these facts, and the deep plans laid by Walkinshaw, it behooves you to obtain from the Supreme Government of Mexico, the *full and positive grant of the two sitios of land upon the mine of New Almaden*, under the date of *the order to Castillero from Castillo Lanzas*, bearing in mind that this grant must express the entire approbation of the Supreme Government of the *concessions made by the local authorities, or Alcaldes*, of the District of San José, of the original grant or *registration of the mine.*

I have not time nor strength to give all these letters. There are various other letters which bear the same interpretation, and nothing else.

My friend, Mr. Randolph, suggested the other day that the letter, to which I am about to advert now, could not have been produced in consequence of what was made known to Forbes; because a copy of that letter is proven to have been in the possession of Mr. William E. Barron about the 1st of July. Now the facts are these. Forbes is examined first on the 14th, and consecutively to the 19th of December, 1857, (page 433 to 490). At that examination he said over and over again, that he had no knowledge of a grant from Castillo Lanzas, nor of the other papers on which we rely. His object was to show that the very grant on which we are relying now, came into existence afterwards; that it was "false, fraudulent, forged and fabricated." My brother, who conducted the cross-examination on the part of the claimant, produced this letter at the examination, and asked him if it was a genuine letter—one written by himself on the 14th of July, 1847. And that letter on its face deals with the grant of the 23d of May, 1846, (Castillo Lanzas grant); admits it. On page 541, you will find that letter. Let me read a word or two from it:

I have the pleasure to communicate to you, that up to the present time nothing has occurred to affect the quiet occupation of the mine of Almaden. * * * * I was presented yesterday with a splendid specimen of quicksilver ore, from a spot *within or near the limits of the two leagues conceded to Castillero and socios.* * * I immediately had an interview with the discoverers, and informed them that if any such vein did in reality exist *without the limits of the two leagues,* and documents would be manifested of the denunciation, I was ready to enter into a contract in the name of the company of Almaden for working the vein, but that I could not permit any claim or operation to be entered upon, until *the land* should be *measured.*

That is to say, until the *two leagues* should be *measured.* So that in this letter he made the admission that, on the 14th of July, 1847, he knew there was a grant of two leagues of land made to Castillero and socios, which is the Lanzas grant. He was called up, and that letter was presented to him, and he tried to get clear of the discovery. He said, on the original examinations all he intended to say was, that he had not seen the *original* papers; that he never meant to deny that he had seen *copies* of the grant! A very intelligent and acute man, as evidenced from his examination!

We called him again on the 30th of July, 1858. The examination will be found on page 837. We produced to him other letters; one dated May 5, 1847. And that letter of the 5th of May, 1847, was not more fatal to the truth of his testimony as given on the original direct examination, than was the letter of the 14th of July, 1847. The letter of the 5th of May, 1847, entered more into detail; that is all.

Well, that whole theory was at an end; that whole scheme is blown up. The conspiracy—or call it by whatever term you think proper—had failed, and promised to fail absolutely. The production of his letter of the 14th of July, 1847, told him that the claimants were in possession of evidence damning to the truth of his own story, and fatal to his own reputation.

He had sworn that he had no knowledge of a grant. The letter of the 14th of July recognizes a *grant* as situated upon the *mining possession ;* for, upon the faith of the grant he admonished those claiming under the Cook title not to interfere with that particular mine until it was ascertained whether it was outside or inside the limits of the concession made to Castillero by the Lanzas grant.

Well, when he comes up again, with that letter before him, he forgets the letter of the 28th of March, 1848. That letter you will find at page 864.

The letters which he had sold to Laurencel before, and for which he had received from Laurencel $20,000, all looked to the obtaining of papers from Mexico. He stated that there were no such papers in existence as the papers which we produce now, and upon which we rely for title. We prove to him by his own letter of the 14th of July, 1847, that, as far back as July, 1847, he admitted the title papers upon which we rely without any question ; that he held the property by virtue of them.

It was evident, then, may it please your Honors, that the title could not have been manufactured in consequence of his suggestions made in 1849.

And then he manufactures this letter of the 28th of March, in which it is said for the first time, and the only time, that the documents procured by Castillero in Mexico were all obtained long after the occupation of California by the Americans. This is dated in March, 1848. The letters of 1849 were utterly inconsistent with the truth of this statement.

He produces a copy of a letter from Alex. Forbes, in which he mentions as a reason why he would not give as much as was asked for some additional interest in the mine :—" that in fact, the documents procured by Castillero in Mexico, as his title to the mine and lands, were all obtained *long after the occupation of California by the Americans."*

That is not referred to anywhere in these letters, may it

please your Honors. On the contrary, as I have just said, the letters which I have read, dated in October and December, and all the other letters on the subject, are inconsistent with the assertion here apparently incidentally made, that all the papers on which we now rely were *fraudulently manufactured*.

But there is another thing in that letter to which your Honors' attention has not been called, which demonstrates itself a forgery, and that is this.

It speaks of a date in 1848, not supposed to be material to the validity of this title. His letters in 1849 suggested only that the papers he desired to obtain should bear the same date as that of the Lanzas decree; that was all. That date was before the occupation of the country by the United States. And *here* he tells us, he makes Alex. Forbes write to him. (Page 864):

The documents procured by Castillero in Mexico, as his title to the mine and lands, were all obtained long after the occupation of California by the Americans.

You may look in vain through this correspondence to find any suggestion that the date of the war was material at all. The war was not *then* supposed to operate upon the grants made after the war was declared. But the time this letter was *forged* it was considered material. I mean to say that on the 28th of March, 1848, the question as to the occupation by the American army, as far as that fact might touch the validity of grants made by Mexico, was not considered material at all. The question had then never arisen. It first came up before Judge Hoffman several years afterwards.

MR. RANDOLPH—Did the people think that these grants could be made *after* the occupation by the Americans?

MR. JOHNSON—Suppose that they did? I do not say that they *could* not. What sort of occupation was it? Did anybody know at the time of that occupation that it was the purpose of the United States to hold on? President Polk said, —and he said it with great truth—that he was anxious to put an end to the war on any terms. He got just about as sick of the war as Mexico did. If Mexico had waited a little longer, perhaps she would not have been compelled to part with California. However, this is out of the case.

MR. RANDOLPH—*Quien sabe?*

MR. JOHNSON—Now it is clear as the sun, that the whole of this case demonstrates the integrity of the title papers upon which we rely; and if, in point of law, these title papers constitute a claim which the Courts of the United States are to respect, because it is a claim which the Mexican Government would have respected, then we are entitled to a confirmation, absolute and unqualified, at the hands of this Court.

I have, I believe, referred to all the matters material to the issues immediately involved in this case.

If the Court will permit me, before I conclude, I desire to refer to a matter personal to myself. I wish to give expression to the very sincere gratification with which, in common with my brother (Mr. Benjamin), we have received the kindness of our brethren of the Bar, and especially the kindness and civility of your Honors upon the Bench; and, what was still more gratifying to us, your courtesies in social life.

MR. RANDOLPH—Do your Honors propose to continue the setting this evening?

MR. JUSTICE MCALLISTER—Do you wish to reply to Mr. Johnson?

MR. RANDOLPH—I feel that it is incumbent upon me to make some reply so far as I may be able to do so. I am very much fatigued, as I suppose the Court are. At the same time I dislike very much to ask anybody connected with this case to come back here on another day of the next week. If your Honors will set this evening I will go on with my reply—if so you prefer.

MR. JUSTICE MCALLISTER—I suppose that on Monday, —being the day before election—the Court will have to set all day to naturalize citizens.

MR. JOHNSON—(*Sotto voce.*) We have quite enough of them already, if their Honors please.

MR. RANDOLPH, (inquiringly)—I had better go on then this evening, sirs?

After consultation the Court ordered an adjournment until Monday, at 2 P. M.